MW00643432

The 30-Day Marriage Challenge

Brad and Laura Engel

Bethel1808 Publishers

The 30 Day Marriage Challenge

Bethel1808

Lewisville, TX 75057

www.Bethel1808.com

ISBNs for The 30 Day Marriage Challenge

Softcover: 978-1-947201-05-7

eBook: 978-1-947201-20-0

Printed in the United States of America

Cover and Interior design: Bethel1808

To Lauren and Stewart,

We have been so richly blessed to have you in our lives for so many years. You have seen our marriage grow from a very bad and hurtful thing into the amazing love that we have today. We pray that the hurtful words that were said and the things that were done by us to each other have no effect on you in your marriages. If any of our baggage was placed upon you, we pray that you be able to drop it and simply love God and love your spouse.

God has such amazing marriages for you both.

He is smiling upon you right now.

We will love you forever.

Love Mom and Dad

Don’t Read This Book!

I’m seriously asking you right now,

"Please don’t read this book straight through."

It is not designed to read in a sitting or even over a couple of days. In fact, it is not designed to be read in less than a month.

This is not an informative, explanatory, teaching-kind of book. You may discover some things that you didn’t already know, but this book is not designed to teach you. It is designed to lead you; and not to someone who can teach you, but to Someone who can change you.

The 30-Day Marriage Challenge is a unique approach to repairing the damage caused by either ourselves or external forces on our marriage. This book is not a typical calendar, marriage-enrichment type of book either. Although it is set with tasks to accomplish nightly, The 30-Day Marriage Challenge is unique. You will not be encouraged to send her flowers at work or leave a cute note on his car window. You will not have romantic homework to try to fan the flames of your intimacy. This book is specifically for those who feel as though they are at the end of their rope; that they are out of options; that only God can save this marriage.

So...what if you’re not falling apart? What if your marriage is not horrible, it is just not great? What if you just feel like roommates passing through life, living together? “At least I am not alone,” you say. This book is also for you.

What about those of us who have great marriages? This book is filled with new and unique ways of seeing and explaining the love of God. There is a word in here that you and your spouse need to hear. And who wouldn’t want a dedicated 90 seconds of their spouse speaking over them every day?

This book will challenge you in ways you cannot imagine. It will push you, stretch you and create a path for love simply by leading and directing you.

Although romantic gestures and deep looks of love are wonderful to do, and we highly recommend them; this book is not about what you can do to save your marriage. In fact, The 30-Day Marriage Challenge is not about you at all...It’s about God.

It is a challenge put to you to let go of who you think your spouse should be and let God show you who they really are, and why He chose this person specifically for you. It is a challenge to release all of your high standards that you have for your spouse and find out that God designed them to far exceed your expectations. It is a challenge to believe that the God who created time and space, light and dark, galaxies and simple blades of grass, knew what He was doing when He gave your wonderful spouse to you and gave you to them. It was no accidental meeting. It was not coincidence. It was designed by a loving Creator who planned all of it out long before you knew Him.

"Before I formed you in the womb I knew you, before you were born I set you apart..."Jeremiah 1:5(NIV)

The 30-Day Marriage Challenge is not designed to read each morning and try to accomplish a goal of "Being Nice Today" or "Focusing on Love." This is not a book of tiny gestures each day that might make your spouse fall in love with you again...no doubt, you have already tried that. You are way past impressing them with a romantic box of chocolates or dedicating their favorite song on the radio.

The 30-Day Marriage Challenge may be the most difficult thing you have ever done, not for your marriage but for your incredible spouse.

That's right. It's not actually about your marriage at all. God didn't give you a marriage...He gave you a friend, a lover, a soul-mate.

In the next 30 days, we are going to get your focus off of yourself and off of the marriage that you are afraid of losing. We are going to get your compass re-calibrated and pointing the right direction; the direction it was pointing when you fell in love and made that decision to spend the rest of your life making your wonderful spouse smile.

Are you ready?

First, you need to know that you are going to fail! That's right. You cannot do this. You know that you have always failed. You make mistakes, you mess up, you sin; and now you have a soul-mate that sees everything that you do. Just because you are married now doesn't mean that you are magically going to stop making mistakes. And you could never be good enough on your own to be worthy of being married to God's favorite child.

Now the good news...it is perfectly okay. In fact, it is designed that way. God created you just the way you are and He is about to show you how He specifically chose you for this relationship, this marriage, this love. I know that you are tired and battle weary, but God has got you. He wants to be a part of this with you and you can't do this without Him...what a great coincidence.

As you fail your way through the next 30 days, do not hang your head in shame. God's beautiful princess is waiting for her knight in shining armor to come rescue her and God's victorious warrior is hoping that he has a princess fighting to hold on and believe in him until he gets there. This is battle! This is war! There is a very real enemy trying to kill you and your beloved. There is no time to feel depressed and lick your wounds. Take up your sword and prepare to defend yourself and your true love from the evil that is attacking. Soon you will not be defending, but advancing the Kingdom God has given you. You will be on the offensive as you take ground back from the enemy that he has stolen.

Kind of sounds a little violent, doesn't it?

It is!

Just look at your spouse. Do they have joy? Are they fully alive, or are they battle-worn and exhausted from fighting a battle that they were not created to fight? Your true love has spent time, energy and resources fighting against the one thing they were trying to reach...you.

And you have done the same. The enemy has created an elaborate system to distract, deceive and disillusion both of you. It's time to clear the smoke and break the mirrors. It's time to see clearly that the two of you are on the same side and are both under attack. There will be plenty of time later to bandage your wounds and relax; but for now, draw your sword, give a barbaric yell and prepare to defend yourself and your wonderful lover from the enemy as you step into...

The

30-Day

Marriage

Challenge.

Table of Contents

My spouse will never do this with me!

That is perfectly okay.

Start where you are. The little bit of energy that you have to give will be joyously accepted by the Lord and multiplied back to your marriage with huge, compounding effects.

Give, and it will be given to you: good measure, pressed down, shaken together, and running over will be put into your bosom. For with the same measure that you use, it will be measured back to you." Luke 6:38 (NKJV)

This journey is not about teaching you how to connect with your spouse. It is about connecting with the One who is already connected to your spouse. You might even think that your spouse is not listening to God.

But God knows them. He created them. He loves them. And He chose them specifically for you.

They are worth fighting for and you have such power in you by the grace and authority of Christ.

***How could one chase a thousand,
And two put ten thousand to flight,
Unless their Rock had sold them,
And the Lord had surrendered them?
Deut.32:30 (NKJV)***

You alone can resist the enemy for your marriage. You can literally chase away a thousand evil demons from attacking you and your spouse. That's huge! And that is without your spouse joining in. Just wait until you see what happens when your loving spouse has rest from the attacks of the enemy because of your commitment. Wait until you see how God can reach them when you resist the enemy and defend them. You don't have to convince your spouse to fight with you or even to support you in this. Let God reach them. You just concern yourself with the job God has commissioned you to do: fight for your spouse.

Rules of Engagement

If this is war, and it truly is, then we need to understand the rules of this war. Adhering to a set of rules does not in any way confine or limit you; it actually sets you free. It enables you to operate in power and authority and allows you to get into the flow of what God is doing. His plan of action is much better than anything we can come up with because He sees the entire picture. He knows how to accomplish the plans that He has for you, plans to bless you.

For I know the plans I have for you," declares the Lord, "plans to prosper you and not to harm you, plans to give you hope and a future. Jeremiah 29:11 (NIV)

The enemy will not obey the rules. The enemy fights dirty and he wants you to fight dirty too. He wants to distract you from listening to God. The enemy wants to get you alone, fighting against him one-on-one and fighting with your lover. He tries to get you to fight about little things, big things, good things and bad things. If he can get you to do it his way, to fight him alone, to be uncovered, then he knows that he can attack you, and also attack your soul-mate.

So let's set some rules of engagement for you and your loving spouse to adhere to together, standing hand-in-hand as you battle the enemy and not each other.

Rule 1. Every Night Before Bed

This is not a quiet time with God. This is not a ritual to do every morning. Marriage is war...not against each other, but actually for each other. You are going into battle to win back the heart of the one you love. Each night you will have a prayer to pray over your loving spouse that you may add to. You will have specific things to pray to cover, anoint, refresh, and revive your soul mate. Over time, your heart will begin to feel again and you will be able to pray, in your own words, a blessing over your Godly spouse.

Rule 2. You Two Alone

NO KIDS! This is not a family session. This is not a play time. This is Ultimate Warfare and not a place for children to be able to distract from what you are speaking over each other and asking God to do. Your children will actually be blessed by having parents that know when it is time to say "No" and focus only on each other. They will be brought into the legacy of love that you are creating for them. No kids. No compromise!

Rule 3. How to Read (Silently)

The reading section for each of you will take approximately 90 seconds. Husbands, you read first. Your beautiful bride will read her page after you and it will take her approximately 90 seconds as well. This is a very important period of time. While your spouse is reading silently, simply watch and think about all the things that originally attracted you to them. Watch their eyes as God begins unfolding revelation to them about how much He loves them. Don't worry about what they are reading; just sit and allow yourself to be awed by them every night. Find something about them that you love and silently thank God for it. And don't get self-conscious as they watch you reading silently when it is your turn. Allow them to notice things and remember why they fell in love with you.

Rule 4. First Into Battle

Husbands, you always pray first. Your beautiful bride is learning to follow you. Lead! This is important as it lets God know that you are ready for the mantle He has placed upon you. It lets the enemy know that he has to deal with the power of God through you and cannot subvert your authority. And it lets your beautiful bride know that you are going to be there with her, leading her.

Rule 5. Be Careful

As you begin this journey, remember that the goal here is to protect each other from harm. You are both vulnerable right now and are learning to trust each other again. You are going to fail. Your loving spouse will most likely see these failures and may even point them out. Let them, but don't wound them during this time. Assume that their guard is down and they want to trust. You have got to be careful with their heart. Watch what you say and even how you say it. Don't ever lash out in prayer against each other or against something that has been done. A harsh word from you while their guard is down can be very destructive. Remember, you are here to help, not hurt.

Rule 6. Surround Her With Love

Husbands, pray last too! Be the first one on the battlefield and be the last one off. Prayer is the battle! Summarize, recount, or reiterate...but finish the prayer time each night by closing it yourself after your beautiful bride prays. Remember, while you are learning to lead, she is learning to follow.

Rule 7. Speak From Your Heart

Husbands, after the prayer is over, you need to let her know that you love her. Every night she needs to hear that this is not just a routine or program to save your marriage. It is a heartfelt attempt to get back the love of your life. This will require vulnerability on your part.

You may get hurt---Be vulnerable anyway! While you are still holding her hands, look at her eyes and say, "I LOVE YOU!" and then just let it sink in. Don't rush.

Wives, after the prayer is over and your amazing husband is telling you that he truly loves you...accept it as real. Don't judge his actions based on your feelings, his degree of sincerity, or even his previous actions. Just believe that what he is saying is true...he loves you. Then, you need to let him know that you love and respect him. He needs to hear it from you. While you are still holding hands, look him in the eyes and say, "I LOVE YOU AND I BELIEVE IN YOU!" and then just let it sink in.

God is about to perform a miracle...

And we want to hear about it!

When you have completed The 30 Day Marriage Challenge, we would love to hear about your experience. We have been praying for you and your marriage and the feedback we get really is a blessing. We love hearing about the things God is doing and how we can continue to be a part of it.

Please email us and let us know about you and your relationship and what has changed. Be as general or specific as you would like and you don't even have to put your name. We never sell, rent or even distribute the information; we simply like to know that we have been a part of what God is doing.

Be sure to tell us all the important details such as how long you have been married, how you met and how much you love each other.

Contact us at:

BradandLaura@Bethel1808.com

Now turn the page and let's see how to complete the challenge!

The Design of the Challenge

Why don't we have two books...
one for her and one for me?

This book has been crafted this way for a purpose. We are going to begin to work together. We are going share. You and your beautiful wife are one. You should have one vision, one focus, one goal. Therefore, you only need one book.

Each night's page for you will work together with the page that is designed for her. Some nights, what you will read silently to yourself will be almost the same as the page that your beautiful bride will read. Some nights, it will be completely different. As the leader, verify each night that you are reading the same numbered topic that she is reading. If for some reason, you get ahead of your beautiful wife, STOP! Go back and read that last day again. It is important that you stay together. Your goal is not to get through this, your goal is to get your beautiful wife through this...not with guilt trips, or condemnation; simply, by leading. She will follow you as you follow God.

If you are leading and she is not following...

THEN YOU ARE NOT LEADING!!!

Stay close, keep it tight and lead by example.

There are light explanations of each night's topic, but they are only that...light explanations. This book is not designed to teach you, it is designed to connect you with the One that can help.

It is very much like having your car towed to a mechanic. It gets dropped off, they will tell you what the problem is and repair it. You do not get to help. You do not get to be taught right there how to fix it yourself. You have to trust the process for repairing your vehicle.

That is how this book is set up. Think of it like the spiritual tow truck that gets you to the right place each night. There are so many tips and techniques that you can learn to help keep this marriage relationship running like a well-oiled engine, but for now...let's get this to the only One who can fix this and put it back into Manufacturer's Specifications.

Commit to the process and watch God do great things with your marriage, your beautiful bride and with you.

Pass this book to your
Beautiful Wife

The Design of the Challenge

Why don't we have two books...
one for him and one for me?

This book has been crafted this way for a purpose.

Your wonderful husband is learning more about how to follow God as he also learns more about how to lead you. This is a time for the two of you to work together. You and your husband are one. You should have one vision, one focus, one goal. Therefore, you only need one book.

Each night's page for you will work together with the page that is designed for him. Some nights, what you will read silently to yourself will be almost the same as the page that your wonderful husband read. Some nights, it will be completely different. As you begin your reading, verify that you are reading the same numbered topic that he is reading. If for some reason, you get ahead of your mighty man, STOP! Go back and read that last day again. It is important that you stay together. Your goal is not to get through this book, your goal is to be lead through this and help him become a good leader...not with guilt trips, or condemnation; simply, by following. Stay close, keep it tight and follow him as he tries to follow God. Remember, God's got this.

There are light explanations of each night's topic, but they are only that...light explanations. This book is not designed to teach you, it is designed to connect you with the One that can help.

It is very much like having your car towed to a mechanic. It gets dropped off, they will tell you what the problem is and repair it. You do not get to help. You do not get to be taught right there how to fix it yourself. You have to trust the process for repairing your vehicle.

That is how this book is set up. Think of it like the spiritual tow truck that gets you to the right place each night. There are so many tips and techniques that you can learn to help keep this marriage relationship running like a well-oiled engine, but for now...let's get this to the only One who can fix this and put it back into Manufacturer's Specifications.

Commit to the process and watch God do great things with your marriage, your amazing husband and with you.

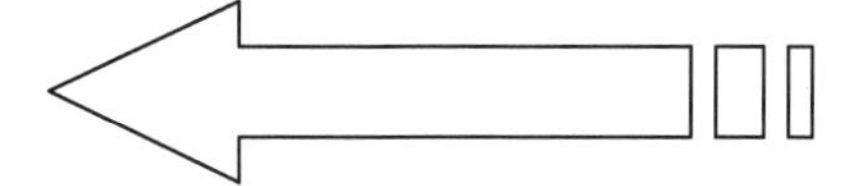

Pass this book back to your
Amazing Husband

Day 1

It actually starts on the next page!!

Day 1
Let's Pray

The next 30 days are going to see some amazing changes...in you, in your beautiful bride and in your marriage. Brace yourself. You are about to be blessed...not by this book or its authors, but by God. I know this because I prayed for it and He told me.

Therefore I tell you, whatever you ask for in prayer, believe that you have received it, and it will be yours.
Mark 11:24 (NIV)

You are about to begin to ask God for a blessing and you are going to believe that He is going to bless you.

In this battle, we have two weapons by which we overcome the enemy: the Word of our Testimony and the Blood of the Lamb, Jesus Christ.

Unfortunately, your marriage doesn't have a very good testimony. You are hurting, you are wounded and you are wounding each other. The enemy is never going to fear and run from an army that is fighting itself.

And you don't understand, or maybe don't fully believe, the power of the Blood of the Lamb. The reason the Blood of our Savior, Jesus Christ, is so powerful against our enemy is because it is Life to us. It is Healing. It is Forgiveness. It is Salvation.

The blood is our eternal defender from anything the enemy has to come against us with.

We access the power of the blood by simply asking for it...through prayer.

The first step is now.

After she reads her page, sit, kneel or stand with your beautiful wife, take her by the hands and pray this prayer over her and your marriage. Then she will pray after you, and you will pray the second prayer to finish up. Don't worry about seeing the results of your prayers. Just trust God. He is faithful and He will come through.

After you close the prayer, before you let go of her hands, look your gorgeous bride in the eyes and tell her...

"I LOVE YOU AND I WILL NEVER STOP LOVING YOU."

Pass this book to your
Beautiful Wife

Day 1
Let's Pray

The next 30 days are going to see some amazing changes...in you, in your loving husband and in your marriage. Brace yourself. You are about to be blessed...not by this book or its authors, but by God. I know this because I prayed for it and He told me.

Therefore I tell you, whatever you ask for in prayer, believe that you have received it, and it will be yours.
Mark 11:24 (NIV)

You are about to begin to ask God for a blessing and you are going to believe that He is going to bless you.

In this battle, we have two weapons by which we overcome the enemy: the Word of our Testimony and the Blood of the Lamb, Jesus Christ.

Unfortunately, your marriage doesn't have a very good testimony. You are hurting, you are wounded and you are wounding each other. The enemy is never going to fear and run from an army that is fighting itself.

And you don't understand, or maybe don't fully believe, the power of the Blood of the Lamb. The reason the Blood of our Savior, Jesus Christ, is so powerful against our enemy is because it is Life to us. It is Healing. It is Forgiveness. It is Salvation.

The blood is our eternal defender from anything the enemy has to come against us with.

We access the power of the blood by simply asking for it...through prayer.

The first step is now.

Sit, kneel or stand with your loving husband as he takes your hands and prays over you. Then, after he prays, pray this prayer over him and your marriage. He will pray one last thing after you. Don't worry about seeing the results of your prayers. Just trust God. He is faithful and He will come through.

After your wonderful husband closes the prayer, before you let go of his hands, look him in the eyes and tell him...

I LOVE YOU AND I WILL ALWAYS BELIEVE IN YOU.

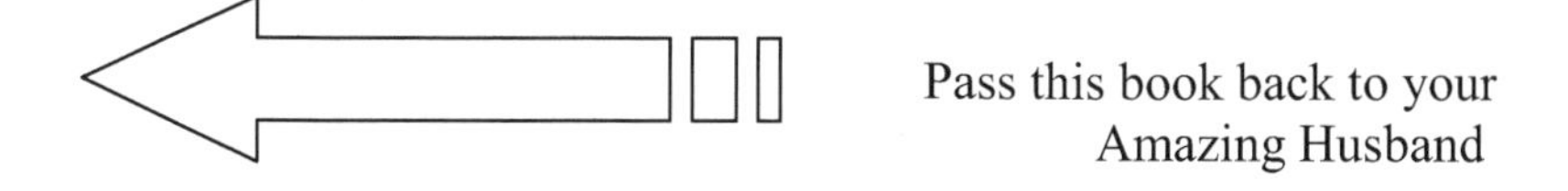

Day 1

Dear God,

I come to You tonight and humbly ask for Your presence in my marriage. I want to put You first and I want You to teach me how to pray for myself, my marriage and most of all, my beautiful wife.

Lord, I ask You for a miracle in my life. I need You and I cannot do this without You. Please come take control of my life and make me a better husband to the woman I love.

Lord, I ask You for a miracle in my marriage. I don't know how to lead my wife. I need You to lead me so that I can lead her. Lord I ask You to begin repairing all the damage I have done. I ask You to help me step aside and allow You to create a loving relationship between my beautiful wife and myself.

Lord, I ask You for a miracle in my wife. She is Your favorite child and You have trusted me to love her. Help her to see my love, even when I don't know how to express it. Bless her with all that You have for her. Show her how beautiful she is and constantly remind her of Your love so she can be confident in You.

Lord, I have made so many mistakes and cannot plead innocent when the enemy says I am guilty. You died and shed your blood for me, so I plead, "Your Blood."

Cover me Lord and let your blood be a powerful weapon in me and my marriage.

(Your beautiful wife prays now.)

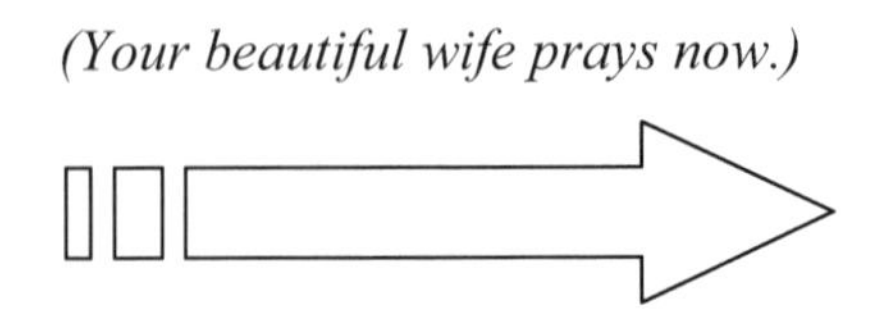

Lord, we stand together tonight and ask for your healing hand on our marriage. We resist the enemy and command him to leave as we submit our lives, our home and our marriage to You.

We stand, praying this in the name of Your Son, Jesus Christ, our Lord; Amen.

Day 1

Dear God,

I come to You tonight and humbly ask for Your presence in my marriage. I want to put You first and I want You to teach me how to pray for myself, my marriage and most of all, my wonderful husband.

Lord, I ask You for a miracle in my life. I need You and I cannot do this without You. Please come take control of my life and make me a better wife to the man I love.

Lord, I ask You for a miracle in my marriage. I don't know how to follow my husband the way You intended. I need You to teach me. Lord I ask You to begin repairing all the damage I've done. Help me step aside and allow You to create a loving relationship between my wonderful husband and myself.

Lord, I ask You for a miracle in my husband. He is Your favorite child and You have trusted me to love and respect him. Help him to see my love, even when I don't know how to express it. Bless him with all that You have for him. Show him how strong he is and constantly remind him of Your love so he can be confident in You.

Lord, I have made so many mistakes and cannot plead innocent when the enemy says I am guilty. You died and shed your blood for me, so I plead, "Your Blood."

Cover me Lord and let your blood be a powerful weapon in me and my marriage.

(Your amazing husband closes in prayer now.)

Day 2
Jesus Loves Me

If you are going to believe God for a miracle in your marriage, the first thing you have to do is believe that...He Loves You.

The truth is that God loves you so much that He did some wonderful things just for you.

First, He created this entire world for you. Each tree that you notice, each blade of grass that you see, and every single star in the sky, even the ones you cannot see, were put there for one reason...you. He was thinking of you when He created the Universe. Think about that for a moment.

Second, because He created you to need Him, He didn't leave you here alone. He is not sitting up in heaven watching us from a distance. He is here...with you. He actually gave up his life for you, and then sent Himself in the Holy Spirit to you so that you can live life...more abundantly.

Then, because He loves you so much, He chose the greatest treasure on earth for you...your beautiful bride. Yes...that's right. She is His greatest creation...the apple of His eye...His favorite daughter. And God loves you so much that He gave her to you to love and bless.

But you think you are totally screwing this up. You think that you are not a good husband and not up to the job of being a good husband. You know deep down that you fail; you sin; you are completely messing this up.

It is perfectly okay!

Actually, He knew that you would mess it up. You have a free will and you don't do everything exactly right. But He gave you that free will. He created you exactly the way He wants you...mistakes and all. You are going to have to learn some things the hard way, but that's exactly how He designed you! He loves that you are free. Free to learn; free to laugh and free to love the way He loves you.

Take a moment and realize that you cannot love your beautiful wife and you cannot correctly feel love from your gorgeous bride unless you know what love is.

The Bible defines love very simply and clearly...

"...because God is love." 1 John 4:8 (NIV)

God loves you no matter what, and He will never stop showing you His love. He loves you so much that he gave you His favorite daughter in marriage. And a great marriage is the outcome of God's love felt by you and passed on towards her; His favorite daughter, your beautiful bride.

Thank Him for His Love.

Day 2
Jesus Loves Me

If you are going to believe God for a miracle in your marriage, the first thing you have to do is believe that...He Loves You.

The truth is that God loves you so much that He did some wonderful things just for you:

First, He created this entire world for you. Each tree that you notice, each blade of grass that you see, and every single star in the sky, even the ones you cannot see, were put there for one reason...you. He was thinking of you when He created the Universe. Think about that for a moment.

Second, because He created you to need Him, He didn't leave you here alone. He is not sitting up in heaven watching us from a distance. He is here...with you. He actually gave up his life for you, and then sent Himself in the Holy Spirit to you so that you can live life...more abundantly.

Then, because He loves you so much, He chose the greatest treasure on earth for you...your wonderful husband. Yes...that's right, your husband is His greatest creation...the apple of His eye...His favorite son. And God loves you so much that He gave this man to you to love and bless.

But you think you are totally screwing this up. You think that you are not a good wife and not up to the job of being a good wife. You know deep down that you fail; you sin; you are completely messing this up.

It is perfectly okay!

In fact, God knew that you would mess it up. You have a free will and you don't do everything exactly right. But He gave you that free will. God created you exactly the way He wants you. Sure, you are going to have to learn some things the hard way, but that's exactly how He designed you!

He loves that you are free. Free to learn; free to laugh and free to love the way He loves you.

Take a moment and realize that you cannot love your amazing husband and you cannot correctly feel love from your wonderful husband unless you know what love is.

The Bible defines love very simply and clearly...

"...because God is love." 1 John 4:8(NIV)

God loves you no matter what, and He will never stop showing you His love. He loves you so much that he gave you His favorite son in marriage. And a great marriage is the outcome of God's love felt by you and passed on towards him, God's favorite son, your wonderful husband.

Thank Him for His Love.

Day 2

Dear Lord,

I just want to thank You for loving me. Thank You for never, ever leaving or giving up on me. Thank You for the love that You have that I don't even understand yet.

Lord, thank You for dying on the cross for me. Thank You that You love me so much that You would give up Your life so that I might live.

I recognize that I make so many mistakes and that I need You. I ask You to come into my life and fill me from the inside out. I want more of Your love and I give my life to You to make me complete.

Thank You for being my Lord and saving me from the pit of hell that I was headed towards.

Help me love my wife the way that You Love me. Help me lead her closer to You. Teach me how to love as I experience more of Your love.

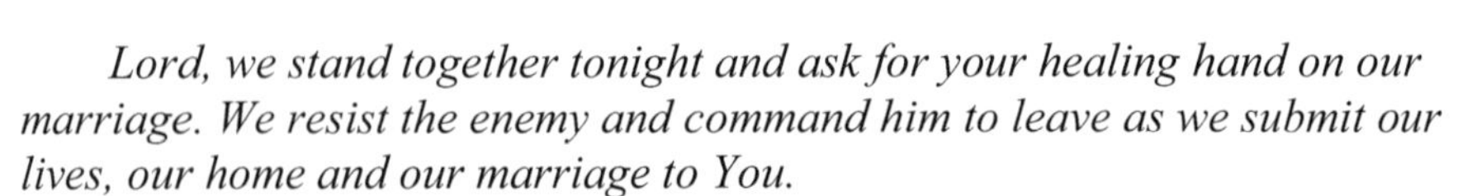

Lord, we stand together tonight and ask for your healing hand on our marriage. We resist the enemy and command him to leave as we submit our lives, our home and our marriage to You.

We stand, praying this in the name of Your Son, Jesus Christ, our Lord; Amen.

Day 2

Dear Lord,

I just want to thank You for loving me. Thank You for never, ever leaving or giving up on me. Thank You for the love that You have that I don't even understand yet.

Lord, thank You for dying on the cross for me. Thank You that You love me so much that You would give up Your life so that I might live.

I recognize that I make so many mistakes and that I need You. I ask You to come into my life and fill me from the inside out. I want more of Your love and I give my life to You to make me complete.

Thank You for being my Lord and saving me from the pit of hell that I was headed towards.

Help me love my husband the way that You love me. Help me follow him as he leads me closer to You. Teach me how to love as I experience more of Your love.

Day 3
Repentance

Don't panic.

Repentance is a good thing. God does not punish us, He corrects us and repentance is how we get to correction.

Think of this life as a journey. We don't know what is ahead, but we have the assurance that if we follow the course laid out for us we will finish highly successful. Unfortunately...we get very distracted. We move to the right or to the left. We see things along the way that slow us down or get us off course. Then it is difficult, even impossible sometimes to find our way back to the correct course. We try to move in the direction we think we should go, but just end up getting more lost.

We check our compass and discover our direction is off just a bit...so we course correct. The destination we are going to is one that you can get to from anywhere, but you have to use the compass and course correct. The more often you course correct, the easier it is to stay on the right road.

Repentance is simply asking God to help us course correct. In acknowledging our mistakes, we give God an opportunity to set us back on the right course. His desire is to help us do this as easily as possible. The longer we go without repentance, the more askew our journey becomes.

And there is no cost or punishment for repentance.

God longs to be a part of your life and He wants to bless you. You are not being brought before a judge for punishment of your evil acts. You are presenting your life before a loving God who already knows about it and asking Him for His help...and He loves being a part of it.

The Lord is not slow concerning his promise, as some regard slowness, but is being patient toward you, because He does not wish for any to perish but for all to come to repentance.
2 Peter 3:9 (NIV)

Repentance is also for your beautiful bride. She needs to know that you realize that you are not perfect. She needs to know that as you are leading her, you are following an almighty God so she can have full confidence in following you.

Allow your gorgeous wife to see that you are a repentant leader.

Day 3
Repentance

Don't panic.

Repentance is a good thing. God does not punish us, He corrects us.

Think of this life as a journey. We don't know what is ahead, but we have the assurance that if we follow the course laid out for us we will finish highly successful. Unfortunately...we get very distracted. We move to the right or to the left. We see things along the way that slow us down or get us off course. Then it is difficult, even impossible sometimes to find our way back to the correct course. We try to move in the direction we think we should go, but just end up getting more lost.

We check our compass and discover our direction is off just a bit...so we course correct. The destination we are going to is one that you can get to from anywhere, but you have to use the compass and course correct. The more often you course correct, the easier it is to stay on the right road.

Repentance is simply asking God to help us course correct. In acknowledging our mistakes, we give God an opportunity to set us back on the right course. His desire is to help us do this as easily as possible. The longer we go without repentance, the more askew our journey becomes.

And there is no cost or punishment for repentance.

God longs to be a part of your life and He wants to bless you. You are not being brought before a judge for punishment of your evil acts. You are presenting your life before a loving God who already knows about it and asking Him for His help...and He loves being a part of it.

The Lord is not slow concerning his promise, as some regard slowness, but is being patient toward you, because He does not wish for any to perish but for all to come to repentance.
2 Peter 3:9 (NIV)

Repentance is also for your wonderful husband. He needs to know that you realize that you are not perfect. He needs to know that you are following him into battle and into repentance as He is trying to follow God so he can have full confidence in leading you.

Allow your wonderful husband to see that you are a repentant woman, standing beside him.

Day 3

Dear Lord,

I just want to come to You tonight and ask You to forgive me.

Lord, forgive me for hurting You. Thank You that You are strong enough to handle all the pain I have caused and gentle enough to love me through all the mistakes.

Lord, forgive me for hurting myself. Forgive me for not loving the way You made me and not honoring You with the life You gave me.

Lord, most of all, I ask You to forgive me for hurting my wife. I ask You to do a miracle in her and remove all the pain and hurt I have caused. I ask You to heal her and help me to bless her and not hurt her. Help me to treat her the way You treat me. Help me to remember that she is Your Princess and now she is my queen. Help me to love her.

Lord I thank You for this opportunity to come to You and get help any time I want. Thank You for leading, guiding and helping me be a better leader, better man and most of all, a better husband to the woman I love.

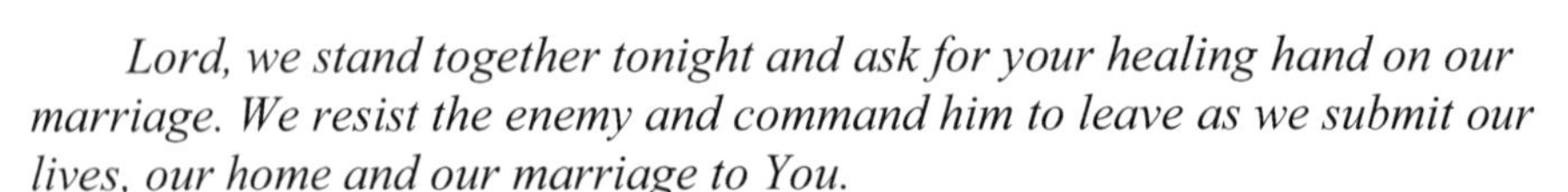

Lord, we stand together tonight and ask for your healing hand on our marriage. We resist the enemy and command him to leave as we submit our lives, our home and our marriage to You.

We stand, praying this in the name of Your Son, Jesus Christ, our Lord; Amen.

Day 3

Dear Lord,

I just want to come to You tonight and ask You to forgive me.

Lord, forgive me for hurting You. Thank You that You are strong enough to handle all the pain I have caused and gentle enough to love me through all the mistakes.

Lord, forgive me for hurting myself. Forgive me for not loving the way You made me and not honoring You with the life You gave me.

Lord, most of all, I ask You to forgive me for hurting my wonderful husband. I ask You to do a miracle in him and remove all the pain and hurt I have caused. I ask You to heal him and help me to bless him and not hurt him. Help me to treat him the way You treat me. Help me to remember that he is Your son and now he is my king. Help me to love him.

Lord I thank You for this opportunity to come to You and get help any time I want. Thank You for leading, guiding and helping me be a better Christian, a better woman and most of all, a better wife to the man I love.

Day 4
Truth or facts

We are conditioned to believe that Truth and facts are the same. In reality, this is not always the case. Many times, what we choose to believe is what we can prove. The facts make it true, Right?

Wrong.

Facts can change; the Truth never changes. This is where faith comes in. This is where we have to choose to believe what God says in spite of the facts.

I feel sick but God says I am healed. (READ--1Peter 2:24)

I am so sinful, but God says I am already forgiven. (READ --Dan 9:9)

I know that I am so dirty, but God says I am clean. (READ --John 15:3)

We have to decide to believe God and we have to determine in our hearts to believe one main thing:

The Word of God is True
no matter what I see, think, feel, hear or say.

Repeat that over and over..

Let that statement really sink in. Make it your mantra for life. Recite it everyday until it becomes your battle cry. Then, believing God for everything else He speaks over you becomes easier.

All Scripture is God-breathed... 2 Tim 3:16 (NIV).

God is not human, that he should lie... Numbers 23:19 (NIV)

The Truth and the facts do not always line up and the facts are almost always easier to believe, but the Truth is always true, always right and always good.

The fact may be that your marriage is struggling. The fact may be that you don't see a solution to this problem with your beautiful wife. The fact may be that this situation with your loving bride looks impossible.

The Truth is that with God all things are possible.

The bible is God's love letter to you. The bible is life and health to you. The bible is God's word and...

No matter what I see,
No matter what I think,
No matter what I feel,
No matter what I hear,
No matter what I say;
...the Word of God is True.

Day 4
Truth or facts

We are conditioned to believe that Truth and facts are the same. In reality, this is not always the case. Many times, what we choose to believe is what we can prove. The facts make it true, Right?

Wrong.

Facts can change; the Truth never changes. This is where faith comes in. This is where we have to choose to believe what God says in spite of the facts.

I feel sick but God says I am healed. (READ --1Peter 2:24)

I am so sinful, but God says I am already forgiven. (READ --Dan 9:9)

I know that I am so dirty, but God says I am clean. (READ --John 15:3)

We have to decide to believe God and we have to determine in our hearts to believe one main thing:

The Word of God is True
no matter what I see, think, feel, hear or say.

Repeat that over and over.

Let that statement really sink in. Make it your mantra for life. Recite it everyday until it becomes your battle cry. Then, believing God for everything else He speaks over you becomes easier.

All Scripture is God-breathed... 2 Tim 3:16 (NIV).

God is not human, that he should lie... Numbers 23:19 (NIV)

The Truth and the facts do not always line up and the facts are almost always easier to believe, but the Truth is always true, always right and always good.

The fact may be that your marriage is struggling. The fact may be that you don't see a solution to this problem with your wonderful husband. The fact may be that this situation with your incredible husband looks impossible.

The Truth is that with God all things are possible.

The bible is God's love letter to you. The bible is life and health to you. The bible is God's word and...

No matter what I see,
No matter what I think,
No matter what I feel,
No matter what I hear,
No matter what I say;

...the Word of God is True

Day 4

Dear Lord,

I come to you tonight and ask you to help me in my unbelief. Help me to determine in my heart to believe You. Lord, help me to believe the Truth in spite of the facts.

Lord, I ask you tonight to lead me into seeing the truth more clearly. Help me to recognize when the facts are not lining up with what you say.

Lord I declare right now that I choose to believe You and your Word over me. You say that I am loved. You say that I am forgiven. You say that I am clean. I know that I fail so many times, but you say I am accepted. I choose to believe You when You say that You see me through the filter of Jesus Christ your Son. No matter what the world says about me, I choose to believe You and your Word. I choose to believe the truth over my life.

Lord I declare right now that I choose to believe You and your Word over my marriage. I choose to believe that you are the head of this union and that You planned this. I choose to believe that You gave me this beautiful woman to be my bride and that You gave me to her to be her loving husband. I choose to believe that You have Blessed this marriage and that You continually look for ways to Bless me, my gorgeous wife, and our wonderful marriage. I choose to believe the truth over my marriage.

Lord, I declare right now, that I choose to believe You and your Word over my wife. You say that she is your precious daughter. You say that she is beautiful. You say that she is a Proverbs 31 woman and that she is exactly the way You created her to be. I choose to believe that You have blessed me with her and that she loves me and is the best wife, friend, lover and encourager I could ever have. I choose to believe the Truth over my beautiful wife.

Lord, we stand together tonight and ask for your healing hand on our marriage. We resist the enemy and command him to leave as we submit our lives, our home and our marriage to You.

We stand, praying this in the name of Your Son, Jesus Christ, our Lord; Amen.

Day 4

Dear Lord,

I come to you tonight and ask you to help me in my unbelief. Help me to determine in my heart to believe You. Lord, help me to believe the Truth in spite of the facts.

Lord, I ask you tonight to lead me into seeing the truth more clearly. Help me to recognize when the facts are not lining up with what you say.

Lord I declare right now that I choose to believe You and your Word over me. You say that I am loved. You say that I am forgiven. You say that I am clean. I know that I fail so many times, but you say I am accepted. I choose to believe You when You say that You see me through the filter of Jesus Christ your Son. No matter what the world says about me, I choose to believe You and your Word. I choose to believe the truth over my life.

Lord I declare right now that I choose to believe You and your Word over my marriage. I choose to believe that you are the head of this union and that You planned this. I choose to believe that You gave me this wonderful man to be my husband and that You gave me to him to be his loving wife. I choose to believe that You have Blessed this marriage and that You continually look for ways to Bless me, my incredible husband, and our wonderful marriage. I choose to believe the truth over my marriage.

Lord, I declare right now, that I choose to believe You and your Word over my husband. You say that he is your son. You say that he is loved, accepted and blessed. You say that he is exactly the way You created him to be. I choose to believe that You have blessed me with him and that he loves me and is the best leader, friend, lover and encourager I could ever have. I choose to believe the Truth over my God-given husband.

Day 5
Brick by Brick

Husbands, love your wives and
do not be harsh with them. Col 3:19 (NIV)

Now you are ready to go to work. You are a powerhouse of spiritual energy and now is when we put all that energy to use for the good of your relationship. However, we are not going to be building anything... we are going to be destroying something.

As with any remodeling job, you have to get rid of anything that doesn't need to be in the finished plans. We are about to allow God to "Remodel" your relationship with your beautiful bride.

This harsh world, all the negative things around her, attacks from the enemy and especially "friendly-fire" have caused her to build a wall around herself for defense. As you try to reach her, you are instantly repelled by this wall. She may not even be aware that she has it there. We all get used to living life within these walls, thinking that we are free when actually we are bound by our own defenses.

It is your job as the leader of this relationship, as her husband, as her lover, to begin implementing and overseeing the safe removal of this wall.

Every time you hurt her just a bit, she adds a brick to her wall. As she gets accustomed to you hurting her, the bricks actually get added two and three at a time. This wall goes up fast because you have become very efficient at the little jabs and hurts. Her beliefs about you and your intentions are what determine the number of bricks added to the wall, and it becomes easy for her to believe that your intentions are not good, whether this is true or not. It is her beliefs that she relies upon here.

Since they are not your bricks, you cannot remove them.

But...every time you bless her, you allow her to remove part of the wall. Some things that you do will not influence her to remove even one single brick, but just wiggle a brick a little. It may take three or four incredible gestures to remove one brick, especially at first. Remember, it is her beliefs that determine how many bricks get moved. As she believes in you more, tiny gestures will remove huge amounts of bricks.

Don't get discouraged.

This wall is huge, and thick, and wide. But you are the Man of God chosen specifically for this task. Soon you and your Gorgeous Wife will be on the same side of the wall working together, standing side by side, with her trusting you completely as you show her how much you love her.

It is coming.

Now let's go tackle that wall.

Day 5
Brick by Brick

Now you are ready to go to work. You are a powerhouse of spiritual energy and now is when we put all that energy to use for the good of your relationship. However, we are not going to be building anything... we are going to be destroying something.

As with any remodeling job, you have to get rid of anything that doesn't need to be in the finished plans. We are about to allow God to "Remodel" your relationship with your loving husband.

This harsh world, all the negative things around him, attacks from the enemy and especially "friendly-fire" have caused him to build a wall around himself for defense. As you try to reach him, you are instantly repelled by this wall. He may not even be aware that it is there. We get used to living life within these walls, thinking that we are free when actually we are bound in our own defenses.

It is your job as his wife, as his friend, as his lover; to begin s implementing and overseeing the safe removal of this wall.

Every time you hurt him just a bit, he adds a brick to his wall. As he gets accustomed to you hurting him, rejecting him, not respecting him, the bricks actually get added two and three at a time. This wall goes up fast because you have become very efficient at the little jabs and hurts. His beliefs about you and your intentions are what determine the number of bricks added to this wall, and it becomes easy for him to believe that your intentions are not good, whether this is true or not. It is his beliefs that he relies upon here.

Since they are not your bricks, you cannot remove them.

But there is good news....

Every time you bless him, you allow him to remove part of the wall. Some things that you do will not influence him to remove even one single brick, but just wiggle it a little. It may take three or four huge gestures to remove one brick, especially at first. Remember, it is his beliefs that determine how many bricks get moved. As he feels your love and respect more and more, tiny gestures will remove huge amounts of bricks.

Above all, love each other deeply, because love covers over a multitude of sins. 1Peter 4:8 (NIV)

Don't get discouraged. This wall is huge, and thick, and wide. But you are the Woman of God chosen specifically for this task. Soon you and your Wonderful Husband will be on the same side of the wall working together, standing side by side, trusting him completely as he shows you how much he loves you. It is coming.

Now let's go tackle that wall.

Day 5

Dear Lord,

I come to you tonight and thank you for loving me enough to take down the wall that I had built around myself. Thank you that you persevered and endured my backlash against you while you were working to reach me. Thank you for removing each and every brick that was in between You and me and that You are so faithful to complete the work that you have started in me.

Lord, I thank you for reaching my wonderful wife and taking down the wall between You and her. I thank you that You never gave up on her and continue to complete the work that you started in this beautiful woman.

Lord, I ask for your help in the task that you have commissioned me to do. I ask you to help me persevere and never quit. I ask you to help me know exactly what to do to allow my gorgeous wife to remove this wall brick by brick. I ask you to give me wisdom in knowing the things to do and the words to say, and how to love my beautiful bride in order for her to feel loved.

I ask you Lord, to help us remove all these bricks from the walls between us. Help me reach her completely, with nothing in between. Help me to show your loving daughter that I want to love her more.

Lord, I ask you to protect her from any bricks I may add while I am learning to take this wall down. Help my beautiful bride to see the good effort that I am doing and help her to not notice the mistakes I continue to make. Help her to not hold my faults against me even though I may deserve it. I ask you Lord to bless my precious wife with so much that it overflows out of her on to everybody around her.

Lord, we stand together tonight and ask for your healing hand on our marriage. We resist the enemy and command him to leave as we submit our lives, our home and our marriage to You.

We stand, praying this in the name of Your Son, Jesus Christ, our Lord; Amen.

Day 5

Dear Lord,

I come to you tonight and thank you for loving me enough to take down the wall that I had built around myself. Thank you that you persevered and endured my backlash against you while you were working to reach me. Thank you for removing each and every brick that was in between You and me and that You are so faithful to complete the work that you have started in me.

Lord, I thank you for reaching my wonderful husband and taking down the wall between You and him. I thank you that You never gave up on him and continue to complete the work that you started in this wonderful man.

Lord, I ask for your help in the task that you have commissioned me to do. I ask you to help me persevere and never quit. I ask you to help me know exactly what to do to allow my wonderful husband to remove this wall brick by brick. I ask you to give me wisdom in knowing the things to do and the words to say, and how to love and respect my incredible husband in order for him to feel loved.

I ask you Lord, to help us remove all these bricks from the walls between us. Help me reach him completely, with nothing in between us. Help me to show your wonderful son that I want to love him more.

Lord, I ask you to protect him from any bricks I may add while I am learning to take this wall down. Help my wonderful man to see the good effort that I am doing and help him to not notice the mistakes I continue to make. Help him to not hold my faults against me even though I may deserve it. I ask you Lord to bless my loving husband with so much that it overflows out of him on to everybody around him.

Day 6
Carry-On

Baggage...we all have it. We all carry things from our past. We hold on to things that have hurt us thinking that if we hold on to them, they can't hurt us again. We don't like our baggage and sometimes pretend that we don't have any baggage, but until we lay it down, we have to carry it.

Your job as a loving husband is to carry your beautiful bride's baggage.

Husbands, in the same way be considerate as you live with your wives, and treat them with respect as the weaker partner and as heirs with you of the gracious gift of life, so that nothing will hinder your prayers. 1 Peter 3:7 (NIV)

She needs to check that baggage with you just as if she were checking it on an airplane. That plane has the job of lifting the baggage off the ground and getting it to the destination. Even if we keep our bags with us as "carry-on," the plane still has the same workload. Your beautiful wife will try to keep her baggage as her own carry-on, thinking she is making your life easier. But when God put you in charge, you now have the responsibility for her baggage.

Don't worry. You are the man that God has specifically chosen to love this beautiful woman and carry her baggage. But you were not designed to carry all of her baggage and yours too.

You truly need to let go of the things you have been holding onto in order to effectively carry your wonderful wife's baggage.

Unfortunately, you cannot lay down your precious wife's baggage...only she can. There is no way for you to change her emotionally, mentally or spiritually. You can only lead her.

But as you lead her in love, she will be able to release some of the baggage that you are carrying. She will let it go as she feels love and protection from you. The more she feels your protection, the less she will need to hold on to her baggage to protect herself. It may be a long journey and all this emotional baggage will be heavy, but you are the right man for the job. God designed you to be able to hold every bit of baggage that she has until she releases it. He did not design you to hold on to your baggage though. He wants you to give it to Him so that you can effectively lead His gorgeous daughter to do the same.

Carrying her baggage for her is an act of love and will be noticed. Maybe not right away, but eventually, it will have compounded effects on your relationship. You can do it. You are strong enough. You are the gate storming, demon-repelling, victorious warrior, man of God that He created you to be.

Lift with your legs, not your back!

Day 6
Checked Baggage

Baggage...we all have it. We all carry things from our past. We hold on to things that have hurt us thinking that if we hold on to them, they can't hurt us again. We don't like our baggage and sometimes pretend that we don't have any baggage, but until we lay it down, we have to carry it.

Your loving husband's job is to carry your baggage. You need to check that baggage with him just as if you were checking it on an airplane. Whether we check it or carry our bags on the plane, it is still the planes job to lift it off the ground and get it to its destination. As the leader of your family, your baggage is his to lift. You may try to keep your baggage as carry-on, thinking you are making your husband's life easier, but when God put him in charge, He gave your loving husband the responsibility for you and all of your baggage.

Your wonderful man has his own baggage that he is trying to let go of, and sometimes his baggage may weigh heavy on you. You truly need to let go of your baggage that you are holding onto in order to effectively help in the vision God has given the two of you.

Unfortunately, your loving husband cannot lay down your baggage...only you can. There is no way for him to change you emotionally, mentally or spiritually. He can only love and lead you.

But as you follow him, you will be able to release some of the baggage that you and he are carrying. The more you feel his love and protection, the less you will need to hold on to your baggage to protect yourself. The more he feels your love and respect, the more he will be able to lay down his own baggage. All this emotional baggage will be heavy, but you are the woman that God has specifically chosen for this job. He did not design you to hold on to your baggage, He designed you to give it to Him so that you can effectively help your loving husband to do the same.

Wives, in the same way submit yourselves to your own husbands so that, if any of them do not believe the word, they may be won over without words by the behavior of their wives...
1 Peter 3:1 (NIV)

Just the act of carrying your baggage for you is an act of love and should be noticed. Your husband loves you enough to carry your baggage for as long as necessary. It is your job to help him be the leader that God made him to be. You are strong enough to release it all to God. You are the gate storming, demon-repelling, woman of God that He created you to be. You are the only woman qualified for this job.

Day 6

Dear Lord.

I come to you tonight and thank you for freeing me from all my baggage. Thank you that you trade yokes with me and that you are willing to take all my baggage upon yourself. Help me Lord to release all my baggage to you as I learn to trust your faithfulness more and more.

Lord I ask you to help me learn to carry my beautiful wife's baggage. Allow me to understand her pain as I lead her closer to you. Help me to be strong even when I am feeling weak. Help me to never hold it against her if she may struggle to release her baggage.

Lord I ask you to give me the things to say and do to help her release her baggage completely. Help me to love her and protect her so that she can see you even more clearly.

Lord I ask you to protect her from me as I learn to carry this baggage. Help her not to see my failings and help her not to feel the sting any time I lash out in anger about any baggage that she is struggling to lay down. Help her to see that I truly want her to be free and that I am willing to carry all of her baggage to the end of the earth so that she would not have to.

Lord, bless her with the ability to trust me by trusting you. Bless her with the confidence in me because she can have confidence in you.

Lord, we stand together tonight and ask for your healing hand on our marriage. We resist the enemy and command him to leave as we submit our lives, our home and our marriage to You.

We stand, praying this in the name of Your Son, Jesus Christ, our Lord; Amen.

Day 6

Dear Lord.

I come to you tonight and thank you for freeing me from all my baggage. Thank you that you trade yokes with me and that you are willing to take all my baggage upon yourself. Help me Lord to release all my baggage to you as I learn to trust your faithfulness more and more.

Lord I ask you to allow me to understand my loving husband's pain and weaknesses as he tries to carry all my baggage that I haven't released. Help me to be strong even when I am feeling weak. Help me to never hold it against him if he struggles to stand with me and carry my baggage.

Lord I ask you to give me the things to say and do to help him release his baggage completely. Help me to love and respect him so that he can see you even more clearly.

Lord I ask you to protect him from me as he learns to carry my baggage. Help him not to see my failings and help him not to feel the sting any time I lash out in anger about any baggage that I may be struggling to lay down or any baggage that he still carries of his own. Help him to see that I truly want him to be free and that I am willing to help all I can.

Lord, bless me with the ability to trust him by trusting you. Bless him with the ability to feel love and respect from me.

Day 7
Scratch and Cut

There is a huge difference in a scratch and a cut, both physically and emotionally. Physically, a scratch is light and a cut is deep. The same is true emotionally.

An emotional scratch is something that may have hurt a bit but wasn't necessarily intentional. An emotional cut is something intentionally designed to hurt.

In your marriage, there are plenty of emotional scratches and cuts, but sometimes, after we have been hurt once, every little scratch feels like a deep, un-healable cut. We begin to judge the intentions and not just look at the actions. Little mistakes that are said or done innocently begin to be seen as intentional wounds. And other times, cuts become the standard operating procedure and we feel cut because we are actually being cut.

The words of the reckless pierce like swords, but the tongue of the wise brings healing. Proverbs 12:18 (NIV)

The more cuts you feel, the easier it is to lash out and cut your precious bride. Most cuts in a marriage are defensive actions to protect ourselves from getting hurt any more.

You need to know that you are being played by the enemy. If he can get you to fight within your own kingdom, his attack is so much easier. There is a solution to this.

The closer you grow in Love with your beautiful bride, the less you will want to hurt her, and the less she will lash out at you in pain. Sounds easy...unless you are fighting, or angry, or upset, or mad, or lethargic or shut down. Actually, it's never easy!

It is your job as the leader to recognize when the enemy is attacking and defend against it. Your bride may still need some time to realize the attack and may still lash out at you instead of focusing her energy against the common enemy.

Let Her!

Remember...she is hurting and some of that pain is due to scratches and cuts from you. Allow her time to see you leading against the enemy and not against her. She will follow your lead as she realizes that you are defending her, not attacking her.

You are tough enough to handle this friendly fire and not fire back or hold it against her. I know this because God gave her to you. He did not make a mistake. He knew you were the perfect man for her and He knew exactly how many cuts and scratches she would aim your way. He gave her to you anyway.

Be the leader and follow God in this.

Day 7
Scratch and Cut

There is a huge difference in a scratch and a cut, both physically and emotionally. Physically, a scratch is light and a cut is deep. The same is true emotionally as well.

An emotional scratch is something that may have hurt a bit but wasn't necessarily intentional. An emotional cut is something intentionally designed to hurt.

In your marriage, there are plenty of emotional scratches and cuts, but sometimes, after we have been hurt once, every little scratch feels like a deep, un-healable cut. We begin to judge the intentions and not just look at the actions. Little mistakes that are said or done innocently begin to be seen as intentional wounds. And other times cuts even become the standard operating procedure and we feel cut because we are actually being cut.

The words of the reckless pierce like swords, but the tongue of the wise brings healing. Proverbs 12:18 (NIV)

The more cuts you feel, the easier it is to lash out and cut your hurting husband. Most cuts in a marriage are defensive actions to protect ourselves from getting hurt any more.

You need to know that you are being played by the enemy. If he can get you to fight within your own kingdom, his attack is so much easier. There is a solution to this.

The closer you grow in Love with your incredible husband, the less you will want to hurt him, and the less he will lash out at you in pain. Sounds easy...unless you are fighting, or angry, or upset, or mad, or lethargic or shut down. Actually, it's never easy!

It is your job to recognize when the enemy is attacking and defend against it. Your husband may still need some time to realize the attack and may still lash out at you instead of focusing his energy against the common enemy.

Let Him!

Remember...he is hurting and some of that pain is due to scratches and cuts from you. Allow him time to see you fighting against the enemy and not against him. He will begin to lead as he realizes that you are defending him, not attacking him.

You are tough enough to handle this friendly fire and not fire back or hold it against him. I know this because God gave him to you. It was not a mistake. He knew you were the perfect woman for him and He knew exactly how many cuts and scratches he would inflict and gave him to you anyway.

Take a step back and defend what's yours.

Day 7

Dear Lord,

I come to you tonight and confess that I am hurting. I ask you to heal me of all my wounds. I ask you to help me to believe fully that my sins, my sickness and all my wounds were healed at the cross. Your word says that you were bruised, beaten and whipped for my healing and I accept all of it.

I ask for your forgiveness for the times that I have lashed out and cut at You. I ask for your forgiveness for the times that I have unintentionally said and done things that were against you.

I ask you Lord to help me be the leader that you created me to be even when I am being hurt.

I ask you Lord to forgive me for hurting your princess, my queen. I ask you right now Lord to heal her heart and help her forgive me for all the times that I cut or scratched her. Help her see my Love, not my anger, pain or mistakes.

I ask you Lord to help me control my tongue and my thoughts. Help me to be quick to speak life over my beautiful wife and refrain from hurtful comments.

I ask you Lord to help me recognize the attacks of the enemy and be quick to defend and protect my wonderful wife. Help me to guard against the fiery darts of the evil one.

Lord, I ask you to help my beautiful Bride see the man that wants to help heal her wounds and not inflict them on her.

Lord, we stand together tonight and ask for your healing hand on our marriage. We resist the enemy and command him to leave as we submit our lives, our home and our marriage to You.

We stand, praying this in the name of Your Son, Jesus Christ, our Lord; Amen.

Day 7

Dear Lord,

I come to you tonight and confess that I am hurting. I ask you to heal me of all my wounds. I ask you to help me to believe fully that my sins, my sickness and all my wounds were healed at the cross. Your word says that you were bruised, beaten and whipped for my healing and I accept all of it.

I ask for your forgiveness for the times that I have lashed out and cut at You. I ask for your forgiveness for the times that I have unintentionally said and done things that were against you.

I ask you Lord to help me be the wife that you created me to be even when I am being hurt.

I ask you Lord to forgive me for hurting your favorite son, my king. I ask you right now Lord to heal his heart and help him forgive me for all the times that I cut or scratched him. Help him see my Love, not my anger, pain or mistakes.

I ask you Lord to help me control my tongue and my thoughts. Help me to be quick to speak life over my wonderful husband and refrain from hurtful comments.

I ask you Lord to help me recognize the attacks of the enemy and be quick to defend and protect my incredible husband. Help me to guard against the fiery darts of the evil one.

Lord, I ask you to help my loving husband see the woman that wants to help heal his wounds and not inflict them on him.

Day 8
Forgiveness

You know you have done some things wrong. The bible calls this sin. So many people today want you to focus on your sin in order to keep you from sinning and therefore you will be a better person. This makes for great religion. In fact, every major religion in the world has a tenet of being a good person and not sinning.

But we aren't interested in religion. We are interested in Relationship, and your relationship with God is such that He does not care about your sin.

Yes, that is right! God does not care about your sin.

God is a God of Righteousness and cannot dwell with sin, yet He lives in you and you are sinful. So God made a way that He can be with you and not your sin...He died for it.

He sent His Son to die on a cross to take away all of your sin. The bible says that He forgave it and remembers it no more.

...as far as the east is from the west, so far has he removed our transgressions from us. Psalm 103:12 (NIV)

That was 2000 years before you were even born; 2000 years before you sinned; 2000 years before the sin that you will commit tomorrow. Let that marinate for a minute!

He forgave it and forgot it so that He could live in you, not in heaven separated from you until you finally become perfect.

Forgiveness is for you, not for God. His part is done. It is that gift, wrapped up and decorated with a bow and just setting there waiting for you to unwrap it. It's free and it's for you. Forgiveness is part of that course-correction as we enjoy this journey with Him.

"But without the religious rules, I might sin!"

You are going to sin. But you need to know, nothing you can do can ever separate you from the love of God. No sin can make Him love you less and no religious list of rules, no matter how well you keep them, can ever make Him love you more. He doesn't need to forgive you, He already forgave you.

Now you are no longer focused on your sin and can focus on His love and sin no longer has a hold on you. You can live free as a forgiven, blessed child of God. As you receive the revelation of forgiveness you will be able to forgive your gorgeous wife much easier and lead her by example into true forgiveness.

God doesn't care about your sin, He cares about you!

Day 8
Forgiveness

You know you have done some things wrong. The bible calls this sin. So many people today want you to focus on your sin in order to keep you from sinning and therefore you will be a better person. This makes for great religion. In fact, every major religion in the world has a tenet of being a good person and not sinning.

But we aren't interested in religion. We are interested in Relationship, and your relationship with God is such that He does not care about your sin.

Yes, that is right! God does not care about your sin.

God is a God of Righteousness and cannot dwell with sin, yet He lives in you and you are sinful. So God made a way that He can be with you and not your sin...He died for it.

He sent His Son to die on a cross to take away all of your sin. The bible says that He forgave it and remembers it no more.

...as far as the east is from the west, so far has he removed our transgressions from us. Psalm 103:12 (NIV)

That was 2000 years before you were even born; 2000 years before you sinned; 2000 years before the sin that you will commit tomorrow. Let that marinate for a minute!

He forgave it and forgot it so that He could live in you, not in heaven separated from you until you finally become perfect.

Forgiveness is for you, not for God. His part is done. It is that gift, wrapped up and decorated with a bow and just setting there waiting for you to unwrap it. It's free and it's for you. Forgiveness is part of that course-correction as we enjoy this journey with Him.

But without the religious rules, I might sin!

You are going to sin. But you need to know, nothing you can do can ever separate you from the love of God. No sin can make Him love you less and no religious list of rules, no matter how well you keep them, can ever make Him love you more. He doesn't need to forgive you, He already forgave you.

Now you are no longer focused on your sin and can focus on His love and sin no longer has a hold on you. You can live free as a forgiven, blessed child of God. As you receive the revelation of forgiveness you will be able to forgive your loving husband much easier and help him by example find true forgiveness.

God doesn't care about your sin, He cares about you!

Day 8

Dear Lord,

I just come to you tonight and thank you for the forgiveness that you gave me. I thank you Lord for the opportunity to be in your presence.

Lord I just thank you for forgiving me of all my sin. Thank you that you love me so much, that you would send your own perfect Son to die a sinner's death so that I could be forgiven.

Thank you, Lord that I don't have to try to be good enough to earn your acceptance and forgiveness. I don't have to be perfect to be with you.

Thank you that your forgiveness covers all of my sin; the sins that I committed in the past, the sin that I commit today and all the sins that I will ever commit in the future; thank you that they are all forgiven.

Thank you Lord that when you forgave all of my sin, you also forgot about all my sin. Thank you that when the devil tries to accuse me, even though I am guilty, I get to be cleared of all the charges because of your forgiveness.

Thank you that when you look at me, you don't see my dirty life. You don't see my mistakes and failures. Thank you, Lord that you only see me through the filter of Your Son, Jesus Christ.

Thank you Lord that your forgiveness makes me want to be a better son to you, a better friend to all and most of all, a better husband to the woman I love. Thank you that you blind my wonderful wife from my darkness and help her see me through love.

Lord, we stand together tonight and ask for your healing hand on our marriage. We resist the enemy and command him to leave as we submit our lives, our home and our marriage to You.

We stand, praying this in the name of Your Son, Jesus Christ, our Lord; Amen.

Day 8

Dear Lord,

I just come to you tonight and thank you for the forgiveness that you gave me. I thank you Lord for the opportunity to be in your presence.

Lord I just thank you for forgiving me of all my sin. Thank you that you love me so much, that you would send your own perfect Son to die a sinner's death so that I could be forgiven.

Thank you, Lord that I don't have to try to be good enough to earn your acceptance and forgiveness. I don't have to be perfect to be with you.

Thank you that your forgiveness covers all of my sin; the sins that I committed in the past, the sin that I commit today and all the sins that I will ever commit in the future; thank you that they are all forgiven.

Thank you Lord that when you forgave all of my sin, you also forgot about all my sin. Thank you that when the devil tries to accuse me, even though I am guilty, I get to be cleared of all the charges because of your forgiveness.

Thank you that when you look at me, you don't see my dirty life. You don't see my mistakes and failures. Thank you, Lord that you only see me through the filter of Your Son, Jesus Christ.

Thank you Lord that your forgiveness makes me want to be a better daughter to you, a better friend to all and most of all, a better wife to the man I love. Thank you that you blind my wonderful husband from my darkness and help him see me through love.

Day 9
Believe the Best

In the midst of marital battle, things are said and done that can cause deep, long lasting pain. Sometimes these things are meant to cause such wounds and sometimes they are not.

The truth is that you love your beautiful, God-given bride and she truly loves you. You may say things trying to be funny, sarcastic or even just to sound intelligent, that ended up digging into her emotionally. You didn't mean to hurt her. You may even apologize for it...but it still hurts.

She does the same to you!

The difference when she does it to you is that you have the opportunity to believe the best about her. You have a chance to assume that she meant no harm. Allow her the freedom to compare you to others, mention your shortcomings and sound intelligent without letting it hurt you. Although these little words and actions really do hurt, you are strong enough to handle it. You are created in God's image and you are a man in love...and Love conquers all.

It (Love) always protects, always trusts, always hopes, always perseveres. 1 Corinthians 13:7 (NIV)

Remember when you were dating, if she accidentally said something hurtful, you assumed that she didn't mean it because she would never say "that."

If there is a chance that she doesn't mean it now, then you should give her the benefit of the doubt. Believe the best about her...that she is a wonderful wife that loves you more than anything else on earth and wants to bless you, please you, love you and try to be everything you want. Your beautiful queen deserves the benefit of the doubt. She needs you to believe the best about her when she says or does the wrong thing unintentionally.

By the way, because you love her, you should believe the best about her even when it was intentional. She will rise to become the Godly woman, wife, lover and friend that you prophesy into her by believing the best about her always.

Take the hurt and pain and give it to God. You are tough enough to handle this and when you feel that you are not...God is!

Day 9
Believe the Best

In the midst of marital battle, things are said and done that can cause deep, long lasting pain. Sometimes these things are meant to cause such wounds and sometimes they are not.

The truth is that you love your wonderful, God-given husband and he truly loves you. You may say things comparing him to others, pointing out his shortcomings or even just trying to sound intelligent, that ended up digging into him emotionally. You didn't mean to hurt him. You may even apologize for it...but it still hurts...whether he admits it or not.

He does the same to you!

The difference when he does it to you is that you have the opportunity to believe the best about him. You have a chance to assume that he meant no harm. Allow him the freedom to be funny, sarcastic and even intelligent without letting it hurt you. Although these little words and actions really do hurt, you are strong enough to handle it. You were created in God's image and you are a woman in love...and Love conquers all!

It (Love) always protects, always trusts, always hopes, always perseveres. 1 Corinthians 13:7 (NIV)

Remember when you were dating, if he accidentally said something hurtful, you assumed that he didn't mean it because he would never say "that."

If there is a chance that he doesn't mean it now, then you should give him the benefit of the doubt. Believe the best about him...that he is a wonderful husband that loves you more than anything else on earth and wants to bless you, please you, love you and try to be everything you want. Your incredible husband deserves the benefit of the doubt. He needs you to believe the best about him when he says or does the wrong thing unintentionally.

By the way, because you love him, you should believe the best about him even when it was intentional. He will rise to become the Godly leader, husband, lover and friend that you prophesy into him by believing the best about him always.

Take the hurt and pain and give it to God. You are strong enough to handle this and when you feel that you are not...God is!

Day 9

Dear Lord,

I come to you tonight and ask you to bless me with the ability to only believe the best about this beautiful woman that you gave me.

I know that I have hurt her intentionally and unintentionally and ask you to cover those wounds for her. Help my gorgeous wife not feel the hurts that I have inflicted upon her.

I ask You Lord to help me be the Man of God that you intended for her to have protecting her, defending her, loving her and pleasing her.

I ask you Father to help me to notice much sooner when I am hurting her with my jokes, sarcasm or other words and actions. Help me to not make her feel bad about herself so that I can feel good about myself. Lord help me bless and love her.

Lord I ask you to help me always default to believing the best about my beautiful wife. Whether her words or actions are intentional or unintentional, I know she loves me. Help me to believe this in the midst of anger or hurt. Teach me to discipline myself to always assume the truth about my beautiful bride...that she loves me.

Lord, we stand together tonight and ask for your healing hand on our marriage. We resist the enemy and command him to leave as we submit our lives, our home and our marriage to You.

We stand, praying this in the name of Your Son, Jesus Christ, our Lord; Amen.

Day 9

Dear Lord,

I come to you tonight and ask you to bless me with the ability to only believe the best about this wonderful man that you gave me.

I know that I have hurt him intentionally and unintentionally and ask you to cover those wounds for him. Help him to not feel the hurts that I have inflicted.

I ask You, Lord to help me be the woman of God that you intended for her to have standing by him, defending him, loving him and pleasing him. Lord, help me to see much sooner when I am hurting him with my words and actions. Help me to not make him feel bad about himself so that I can feel good about myself.

Lord, show me how to help him be the best that he can be.

Lord I ask you to help me always default to believing the best about my amazing prince. Whether his words or actions are intentional or unintentional, I know he loves me. Help me to believe this in the heat of anger or hurt. Teach me to discipline myself to always assume the truth about my wonderful husband...that he loves me.

Day 10
Son or Slave

In the Kingdom of God there are only two positions; slave or son. If you are going to live in the palace, those are the only two options you have and they are almost identical...almost.

Slaves get to live in the lap of luxury...so do sons.
Slaves have a job to do...so do sons.
Slaves get to see the Master personally...so do sons.

But then there are the differences.

Slaves get rewarded and punished for good and bad work.
Sons do not get rewards because they understand that it is all their inheritance. Sons never get punished. Sons get disciplined and understand that it is for their good.
Slaves exist in the palace as long as they are useful.
Sons live in the palace because it is their home.
Slaves see the Master and fear Him while standing at attention.
Sons see the Master, but know Him and call Him Daddy.
Slaves present their work to the Master to be approved.
Sons are approved in spite of their work or lack there of.
The bible says,

Therefore you are no longer a slave, but a son, and if a son, then an heir of God through Christ. Galatians 4:7 (NKJV)

When your identity is in Christ, as a son, you can live different. There are still consequences for sin but your sin cannot change your DNA. You are a son and nothing can separate you from the love of God.

You have the option of living as a son or a slave. If you choose to work your way into approval, God must honor that choice and hold you accountable to that standard. Or you can simply accept the approval based on the life, death and resurrection of Jesus Christ. It is your choice.
Your wife is being lead by you. Lead her into Sonship, not into slavery.

Day 10
Son or Slave

In the same way that men are identified as the "Bride of Christ," women are identified as "Sons of God." In the Kingdom of God there are only two positions; slave or son. If you are going to live in the palace, those are the only two options you have and they are almost identical...almost.

Slaves get to live in the lap of luxury...so do sons.
Slaves have a job to do...so do sons.
Slaves get to see the Master personally...so do sons.

But then there are the differences.

Slaves get rewarded and punished for good and bad work.
Sons do not get rewards because they understand that it is all their inheritance. And sons never get punished. Sons get disciplined and understand that it is for their good.
Slaves exist in the palace as long as they are useful.
Sons live in the palace because it is their home.
Slaves see the Master and fear Him while standing at attention.
Sons see the Master, but know Him and call Him "Daddy."
Slaves present their work to the Master to be approved.
Sons are approved in spite of their work or lack there of.
The bible says,

Therefore you are no longer a slave, but a son, and if a son, then an heir of God through Christ. Galatians 4:7 (NKJV)

When your identity is in Christ as a son, you can live different. There are still consequences for sin but your sin cannot change your DNA. You are a son and nothing can separate you from the love of God.

You have the option of living as a son or a slave. If you choose to work your way into approval, God must honor that choice and hold you accountable to that standard. Or you can simply accept the approval based on the life, death and resurrection of Jesus Christ. It is your choice.

Your husband holds your counsel in highest regard. Empower him to live as a son, not a slave.

Day 10

Dear Lord,

I come to you tonight and ask you to help me understand my inheritance. Help me to understand what it means to be your son. Lord I ask you to teach me how to let go of trying to be good enough to please you. Teach me how to just be your son.

Lord I ask you to reveal to me all the blessing that comes with being a son. Show me how much you love me just because You are a Loving Father and not because of anything I have done or will ever do.

Lord, right now, I choose to receive your word over me that I am a son in your kingdom instead of a slave working for you. I cast off all the rules and regulations of being a slave and boldly approach you, knowing that you look at me as my daddy, not my master to be feared.

Lord I ask you to teach my beautiful wife about her position in Christ. Teach her that she is approved of simply because You love her. Help me lead her into being the child of God that you created her to be. Help me treat her as a member of your Royal Family. Help me to lead her into knowing all the peace and joy that comes to her as your daughter. Set her free from all the rules and regulations required of slaves.

Lord, I thank you that you made a way for my gorgeous bride and me to become children in your Royal Family. Thank you that you chose us and that it is not any of our own work that causes us to be in your family.

Lord, we stand together tonight and ask for your healing hand on our marriage. We resist the enemy and command him to leave as we submit our lives, our home and our marriage to You.

We stand, praying this in the name of Your Son, Jesus Christ, our Lord; Amen.

Day 10

Dear Lord,

I come to you tonight and ask you to help me understand my inheritance. Help me to understand what it means to be your child. Lord I ask you to teach me how to let go of trying to be good enough to please you. Teach me how to just be your child.

Lord I ask you to reveal to me all the blessing that comes with being a son. Show me how much you love me just because You are a Loving Father and not because of anything I have done or will ever do.

Lord, right now, I choose to receive your word over me that I am a son in your kingdom instead of a slave working for you. I cast off all the rules and regulations of being a slave and boldly approach you, knowing that you look at me as my daddy, not my master to be feared.

Lord I ask you to teach my wonderful husband about his position in Christ. Teach him that he is approved of simply because You love him. Help me empower him into being the child of God that you created him to be. Help me treat him as a member of your Royal Family. Help me to counsel him into knowing all the peace and joy that comes to him as your son. Set him free from all the rules and regulations required of slaves.

Lord, I thank you that you made a way for my incredible husband and me to become children in your Royal Family. Thank you that you chose us and that it is not any of our own work that causes us to be in your family.

Day 11
Authority

Have you ever wondered why sometimes it seems that your prayers go unanswered?

Have you noticed that sometimes you feel out of your element spiritually; you feel like you are in over your head?

Many times it has to do with our Authority.

When you stepped into being a son, you were given a huge level of authority: authority to heal the sick, cleanse the diseased, cast out demons and even raise the dead. In fact, your authority is so vast, that the demons fear you, as they should.

But often times we don't operate in our authority. It may be because we don't know the authority that we have or simply that we don't believe that we have any authority at all. The enemy loves to play mind games with us and convince us that we don't really have any authority. But you need to know one thing....

You have authority over your marriage.

But I want you to know that the head of every man is Christ, the head of woman is man, and the head of Christ is God.
1 Corinthians 11:3 (NKJV)

You have been commissioned by God, the maker of heaven and earth, to lead your family, your marriage, your wife. He would never position you as the leader without giving you the authority to accomplish the task. Your authority comes from Him because He is Authority. You are His son and He gives you the right, responsibility and relationship to be the best husband possible to the woman you love, his princess; your queen. You cannot fail, unless you do nothing. If you choose not to operate in authority, then it is as good as not having authority. The enemy will only submit to the level of authority that you hold; the level of authority that you know you have; the level of authority that you believe.

The badge that a police officer carries is a symbol of the authority given to him by the governing body. If he sees a crime being committed, and does nothing, he still has the authority; but is choosing not to operate in it. Therefore crime can be continued until he recognizes the authority he holds and exercises it.

Your marriage is one area in which you have absolute authority in Christ to resist the enemy. You have the badge and He is the power behind it. Step into your God-given authority and defend, protect, love, and pray for your beautiful bride.

Day 11
Authority

Have you ever wondered why sometimes it seems that your prayers go unanswered?

Have you noticed that sometimes you feel out of your element spiritually; you feel like you are in over your head?

Many times it has to do with our Authority.

When you stepped into being a son, you were given a huge level of authority: authority to heal the sick, cleanse the diseased, cast out demons and even raise the dead. In fact, your authority is so vast, that the demons fear you, as they should.

But often times we don't operate in our authority. It may be because we don't know the authority that we have or simply that we don't believe that we have any authority at all. The enemy loves to play mind games with us and convince us that we don't really have any authority. But you need to know one thing....

You have authority over your marriage.

The wife does not have authority over her own body, but the husband does. And likewise the husband does not have authority over his own body, but the wife does. 1 Corinthians 7:4 (NKJV)

You have been commissioned by God, the maker of heaven and earth, to protect your family, your marriage, your husband. God would never position you here without giving you the authority to accomplish the task. Your authority comes from Him because He is Authority. You are His favorite child and He gives you the right, responsibility and relationship to be the best wife possible to the man you love, his son; your husband. You cannot fail, unless you do nothing. If you choose not to operate in authority, then it is as good as not having authority. The enemy will only submit to the level of authority that you hold; the level of authority that you know you have; the level of authority that you believe.

The badge that a police officer carries is a symbol of the authority given to him by the governing body. If he sees a crime being committed, and does nothing, he still has the authority; but is choosing not to operate in it. Therefore crime can be continued until he recognizes the authority he holds and exercises it.

Your marriage is one area in which you have absolute authority in Christ to resist the enemy. You have the badge and He is the power behind it. Step into your God-given authority and defend, protect, love, and pray for your wonderful husband.

Day 11

Dear Lord,

I come to you tonight and Thank you for your authority that I am under. I thank you for loving me enough to pull me into your family and for giving me the authority that I have.

Lord, I ask you to help me understand my authority more and more. Give me wisdom as I go to know what you are saying and what you are doing. Help me to operate under your authority.

Lord, Thank you for the authority over my marriage. I hereby declare that my Marriage is off limits to the enemy. I declare that he shall have no right or privilege in this marriage. I know mistakes have been made in the past and may be made in the future, but I choose to accept the authority given me and state plainly that all attacks on this marriage will stop now under the authority given to me in the name of Jesus Christ, my Lord.

Lord I thank you for the authority over my beautiful wife. I hereby declare that she is off limits to the enemy in every way. I declare that he shall have no rights or privilege with her as she is under my authority as I am under Christ's. I choose to accept the authority given to me over her and plainly state that all the attacks on her will stop now, by the authority given to me by Jesus Christ.

Lord, we stand together tonight and ask for your healing hand on our marriage. We resist the enemy and command him to leave as we submit our lives, our home and our marriage to You.

We stand, praying this in the name of Your Son, Jesus Christ, our Lord; Amen.

Day 11

Dear Lord,

I come to you tonight and Thank you for your authority that I am under. I thank you for loving me enough to pull me into your family and for giving me the authority that I have.

Lord, I ask you to help me understand my authority more and more. Give me wisdom as I go to know what you are saying and what you are doing. Help me to operate under your authority.

Lord, Thank you for the authority over my marriage. I hereby declare that my Marriage is off limits to the enemy. I declare that he shall have no right or privilege in this marriage. I know mistakes have been made in the past and may be made in the future, but I choose to accept the authority given me and state plainly that all attacks on this marriage will stop now under the authority given to me in the name of Jesus Christ, my Lord.

Lord I thank you for the authority of my wonderful husband. I hereby declare that he is off limits to the enemy in every way. I declare that the enemy shall have no rights or privilege with him as he is under Christ's authority. I choose to accept the authority given to me for him and plainly state that all the attacks on him will stop now, by the authority given to me by Jesus Christ.

Day 12
Passing Authority

God gives you authority in your marriage and He always backs you up. When you choose to step into your authority, you choose to operate in God and He always covers you. God has given you this authority, even though He knows you are still learning to use it. You may make mistakes, but God is big enough to handle them.

In the same way that God allows you to operate in His authority without requiring perfection, you need to allow your beautiful bride to operate in your authority, and always back her up.

When you placed a ring on her finger, you gave her the right to operate and make decisions for the good of you and your family. That authority given to her must always be enforced in public. She has to know that you are going to protect her even if she makes a mistake.

If mistakes are made, you can pull her aside later, in private and gently correct the situation in love. But you can never uncover her without causing serious harm. She has to know that she will always be covered, even when she is wrong. Otherwise, she will stop operating in that authority for fear of being left alone to defend herself.

This is how God treats us. He will never leave you; He will never fail you, even when you fail Him, even when you are wrong.

Be strong and courageous. Do not be afraid or terrified because of them, for the Lord your God goes with you; He will never leave you nor forsake you. Deuteronomy 31:6 (NKJV)

He will always be there by your side to help you recover. He never embarrasses you in public. You may go so far as to embarrass yourself, but even then He is there to love you through it.

When your beautiful bride steps out and makes decisions for you, your family or your life, support her and allow her the opportunity to learn how to know what decision you would have made in each situation. Allow her to learn to hear your voice in her head; the same way your loving father allows you to learn to hear His.

Day 12
Passing Authority

God gives you authority in your marriage and He always backs you up. When you choose to step into your authority, you choose to operate in God and He always covers you. God has given you this authority, even though He knows you are still learning to use it. You may make mistakes, but God is big enough to handle them.

In the same way that God allows you to operate in His authority without requiring perfection, you need to allow your incredible husband to operate in his authority, and always back him up.

When you placed a ring on his finger, you told the world that you choose to follow him. You gave him the right to operate and make decisions for the good of you and your family. That authority given to him must always be enforced in public. He has to know that you are going to stand by him even if he makes a mistake.

If mistakes are made, you can pull him aside later, in private and gently let him know you disagree. But you can never uncover him without causing serious harm. He has to know that he will always be covered, even when he is wrong. Otherwise, he will stop operating in that authority for fear of being left alone to defend himself.

This is how God treats us. He will never leave you; He will never fail you, even when you fail Him, even when you are wrong.

Be strong and courageous. Do not be afraid or terrified because of them, for the Lord your God goes with you; He will never leave you nor forsake you. Deuteronomy 31:6 (NKJV)

He will always be there by your side to help you recover. He never embarrasses you in public. You may go so far as to embarrass yourself, but even then He is there to love you through it.

When your wonderful husband steps out and makes decisions for you, your family or your life, support him and allow him the opportunity to learn how to know what decision you would have made in each situation. Allow him to learn to hear your voice in his head; the same way your loving father allows you to learn to hear His.

Day 12

Dear Lord,

I come to you tonight and ask you to help me learn to always support my wife.

Help me to know how to give her authority to operate in the areas that she is over. Help me to support her in all the areas in which she moves.

Lord, help me to allow her to make mistakes with her authority and help me know how to show her, in love, the decision I would have made.

Lord, help me to know how to be her authority without abusing that position. Help me to always operate in her best interest and to treat her the way You treat me.

Lord, help me to always stand by my wonderful wife in every situation and never leave her to fend for herself. Help me to always cover her and protect her from anything coming against her.

Help me to teach her more about the authority that she can operate in.

Lord, we stand together tonight and ask for your healing hand on our marriage. We resist the enemy and command him to leave as we submit our lives, our home and our marriage to You.

We stand, praying this in the name of Your Son, Jesus Christ, our Lord; Amen.

Day 12

Dear Lord,

I come to you tonight and ask you to help me learn to always support my wonderful husband.

Help me to know how to give him authority to operate in the areas that he is over. Help me to support him in all the areas in which he moves.

Lord, help me to allow him to make mistakes with his authority and help me know how to show him, in love, the decision I would have made.

Lord, help me to know how to be under his authority and operate in that authority without abusing that position. Help me to always operate in his best interest and to treat him the way You treat me.

Lord, help me to always stand by my wonderful husband in every situation and never leave him to fend for himself. Help me to always cover him and protect him from anything coming against him.

Help me to support him as he learns more about the authority that he can operate in.

Day 13
Rings

That is such a beautiful ring on her left hand. It is so classy and ornate. The diamonds just sparkle. It is the perfect ring for her hand. But it didn't used to be....

The ring that she wears comes from a tradition of sonship. A ring was given to each member of the family to signify that they had the authority of the family. You could see a person's ring and know that they belong to a certain family because they had been given that symbol.

So that's your ring, not hers. In marriage, when you placed your ring on your beloved wife's finger, it declared to the world that when she speaks, it is as good as your word. It said that you will be responsible for any deals that she makes. It declares your complete trust in her.

Women never used to pick out their own rings, because it was an honor to wear the ring of the man that owns your heart. Rings were not feminine at all, but rather large and masculine. Whether your beautiful bride picked out her own ring or you picked it out for her, you placed it on her finger symbolizing that she belongs to you. She is not her own any longer.

And the ring on your finger says the same about you; you belong to her. She will stand by you, pray for you, follow you and in many ways defend you. You are hers.

The wife does not have authority over her own body, but the husband does. And likewise the husband does not have authority over his own body, but the wife does. 1 Corinthians 7:4 (NKJV)

Wear her ring proudly and tell her often how much it means to have it on your finger. Explain to her that you are honored that she chose to wear your ring. Tell her how beautiful her hand is wearing your ring and give her the confidence to be proud of it; not because it is the biggest, most beautiful ring she has ever seen; but because it is yours.

Make a loving prophetic comment every time you see your ring on her finger. Let this trigger a statement in you... "I love you" or "You are the most beautiful lady in the world." Take each opportunity to speak life over her and prophesy over her. Speak the words that God says about you: words of love.

Day 13
Rings

That is such a beautiful ring on your left hand. It is so classy and ornate. The diamonds just sparkle. It is the perfect ring for your hand. But it didn't used to be....

The ring that you wear comes from a tradition of sonship. A ring was given to each member of the family to signify that they had the authority of the family. You could see a person's ring and know that they belong to a certain family because they had been given that symbol.

So that is actually your husband's ring on your left hand, not yours. In marriage, when your loving husband placed his ring on your finger, it declared to the world that when you speak, it is as good as his word. It said that he will be responsible for any deals that you make. It declares his complete trust in you.

Women never used to pick out their own rings, because it was an honor to wear the ring of the man that owns your heart. Rings were not feminine at all, but rather large and masculine. Whether you picked out your own ring or your loving husband picked it out for you, he placed it on your finger symbolizing that you belong to him. You are not your own any longer.

And the ring on his finger says the same about him; He belongs to you. He will stand by you, pray for you, lead you and in many ways defend you. He is yours.

The wife does not have authority over her own body, but the husband does. And likewise the husband does not have authority over his own body, but the wife does. 1 Corinthians 7:4 (NKJV)

Wear his ring proudly and tell him often how much it means to have it on your finger. Explain to him that you are honored that he chose you to wear his ring. Tell him how beautiful his ring is and be proud of it; not because it is the biggest, most beautiful ring you have ever seen; but because it is his.

Make a loving prophetic comment every time you see his ring on your finger. Let this trigger a statement in you... "I love you" or "You are the most wonderful husband in the world." Take each opportunity to speak life over him and prophesy over him. Speak the same words that God says about you: words of love.

Day 13

Dear Lord,

I come to you tonight and thank you for the wonderful woman that you gave me to wear my ring.

I thank you for the way you love me and take ownership of my life. I thank you that you call me into your family and spiritually place a royal robe around me and a spiritual ring on my finger telling the heavens and the earth that I belong to you. You stand for me even when I mess up and allow me the chance to learn how to be a member of your family. You count me as a full son from the moment I entered. Thank you for the way you love me.

Lord, help me to love my beautiful wife the way you love me. Teach me about the deep meanings of placing my ring on her finger and placing her ring on mine. Help me be a great leader to her and allow her to make mistakes while I love her through them. Help me to be the man that she wants and needs in her life. Make me a better husband to her as she proudly wears my ring.

Lord, help me to be the man of God that you have called me to be for her. Lord, make me the best man for her ring to be placed on. Give me the words to say to encourage her and lead her as I strive to impress her. Help me to never stop trying to bring joy to her life.

Lord, I pray that you would bless her in all that she does. Help her to be confident in wearing my ring, knowing that I will enforce her words as if they were my own. Help her to know that as I fail, she can trust You in me and You in spite of me. Help me to make her proud to wear my ring.

Lord, we stand together tonight and ask for your healing hand on our marriage. We resist the enemy and command him to leave as we submit our lives, our home and our marriage to You.

We stand, praying this in the name of Your Son, Jesus Christ, our Lord; Amen.

Day 13

Dear Lord,

I come to you tonight and thank you for the wonderful man that you gave me to give me his ring and to wear mine.

I thank you for the way you love me and take ownership of my life. I thank you that you call me into your family and spiritually place a royal robe around me and a spiritual ring on my finger telling the heavens and the earth that I belong to you. You stand for me even when I mess up and allow me the chance to learn how to be a member of your family. You count me as a full son from the moment I entered. Thank you for the way you love me.

Lord, help me to love my amazing husband the way you love me. Teach me about the deep meanings of placing his ring on my finger and placing my ring on his hand. Help me follow his leadership and allow him to make mistakes while I love him through them. Help me to be the woman of God that he wants and needs in his life. Make me a better wife, lover and friend to him as I proudly wear his ring and he wears mine.

Lord, help me to be the woman of God that you have called me to be for him. Lord, make me the best woman for his ring to be placed on. Give me the words to say to encourage my amazing husband as I strive to bless him. Help me to never stop trying to bring joy to his life.

Lord, I pray that you would bless him in all that he does. Help him to be confident in wearing my ring, knowing that I will always stand by him against anything that comes against us. Help him to know that as I fail, he can trust You in me and You in spite of me. Help him to know that I am proud to wear his ring and help me to make him proud to wear my ring.

Day 14
Why Were You Created?

You have one job to do. You have one responsibility. Until you get this one right, nothing else matters. You may lead a Fortune500 company or have a big house and new car. You may even spend all your time feeding the poor and visiting those in prison; but if you don't get the foundation right, you are building on unstable ground.

There are so many things in life that we can be a part of that will be of benefit to the world around us, but your first priority is to be a... wait for it...

HUSBAND.

Yes, God gave you a mantle of leadership in your marriage; it is a commission to love your beautiful bride with all that is in you. The good news is that you were created to love. You were created to be the husband to the beautiful daughter of God that He gave to you.

It was not coincidence that you found each other. It was not just merely happenstance. She was specifically designed with you in mind. God knew you and knew how He created you, and He created this gorgeous girl just for you. He created her to respond to your love and to love you.

God specifically designed you with her in mind. God knew exactly how He made her and He created you for His precious daughter.

Before I formed you in the womb I knew you, before you were born I set you apart; Jeremiah 1:5 (NIV)

Simply put...you fit together.

As you come to the realization that, before He created you and your beautiful bride, God knew that you would be perfect for each other; then you can be free to love her with all your heart because you know she is designed to accept it. You don't have to worry about God being jealous of your affection for your wife. Your love for her does not diminish the love that you have for God.

Remember, she is His daughter. He wants the best for her and He said that is you. He wouldn't give her to just anybody and He wouldn't want her to live with less love just so that you can love Him more.

Loving your beautiful wife honors God.

Day 14
Why Were You Created?

You have one job to do. You have one responsibility. Until you get this one right, nothing else matters. You may lead a Fortune500 company or have a big house and new car. You may even spend all your time feeding the poor and visiting those in prison; but if you don't get the foundation right, you are building on unstable ground.

There are so many things in life that we can be a part of that will be of benefit to the world around us, but your first priority is to be a... wait for it...

WIFE.

Yes, God gave you a mantle of leadership in your marriage; it is a commission to love your wonderful husband with all that is in you. The good news is that you were created to love. You were created to be the beautiful wife to the loving man of God that He gave to you.

It was not coincidence that you found each other. It was not just merely happenstance. He was specifically designed with you in mind. God knew you and knew how He created you, and He created this wonderful man just for you. He created him to respond to your love and to love you.

God specifically designed you with him in mind. God knew exactly how He made him and He created you to match perfectly with this wonderful man.

Before I formed you in the womb I knew you, before you were born I set you apart; Jeremiah 1:5 (NIV)

Simply put...you fit together.

As you come to the realization that before He created you and your loving husband, God knew that you would be perfect for each other; then you can then be free to love him with all your heart because you know he is designed to accept it. You don't have to worry about God being jealous of your affection for your husband. Your love for him does not diminish the love that you have for God.

Remember, your wonderful husband is His son. God wants the best for him and He said that is you. God wouldn't give him to just anybody and He wouldn't want your husband to live with less love just so that you can love Him more.

Loving your incredible husband honors God.

Day 14

Dear Lord,

I come to you tonight and thank you for a wonderful woman that you created just for me.

I thank you for the gift of her love and affection.

Lord I thank you for her beauty and grace. I thank you that you created her to stir up my emotions and desires.

Lord I thank you that she makes me want to strive to be a better man.

Lord I ask you to help me spend my life doing the one thing you asked of me: Loving, Honoring and Cherishing your precious daughter. I ask for you help in becoming the man of God that she should have.

Lord I pray that you would bless my wonderful wife with the knowledge of love. Help her to know the love that you have for her and help her to know that I love her with all my heart.

Thank you Lord that I can give her my whole heart; and doing that only strengthens my love for you. Help me to understand your love and that when I love her more, I love You more.

Lord, Bless my Beautiful Bride with peace in our relationship. Help her to see that I love her and that she can rest in that love.

Lord Bless my wonderful wife with joy. May my love bring her happiness and laughter. Help her to enjoy being my wife.

Lord, we stand together tonight and ask for your healing hand on our marriage. We resist the enemy and command him to leave as we submit our lives, our home and our marriage to You.

We stand, praying this in the name of Your Son, Jesus Christ, our Lord; Amen.

Day 14

Dear Lord,

I come to you tonight and thank you for a wonderful man that you created just for me.

I thank you for the gift of his love and affection.

Lord I thank you for his strength and passion. I thank you that you created him to stir up my emotions and desires.

Lord I thank you that he makes me want to strive to be a better wife, lover and friend.

Lord I ask you to help me spend my life doing the one thing you asked of me: Loving, Honoring and Respecting your amazing son. I ask for you help in becoming the woman of God that he should have.

Lord I pray that you would bless my wonderful husband with the knowledge of love. Help him to know the love that you have for him and help him to know that I love him with all my heart.

Thank you Lord that I can give him my whole heart; and doing that only strengthens my love for you. Help me to understand your love and that when I love him more, I love You more.

Lord, Bless my incredible husband with peace in our relationship. Help him to see that I love him and that he can rest in that love.

Lord Bless my amazing man with joy. May my love bring him happiness and laughter. Help him to enjoy being my husband.

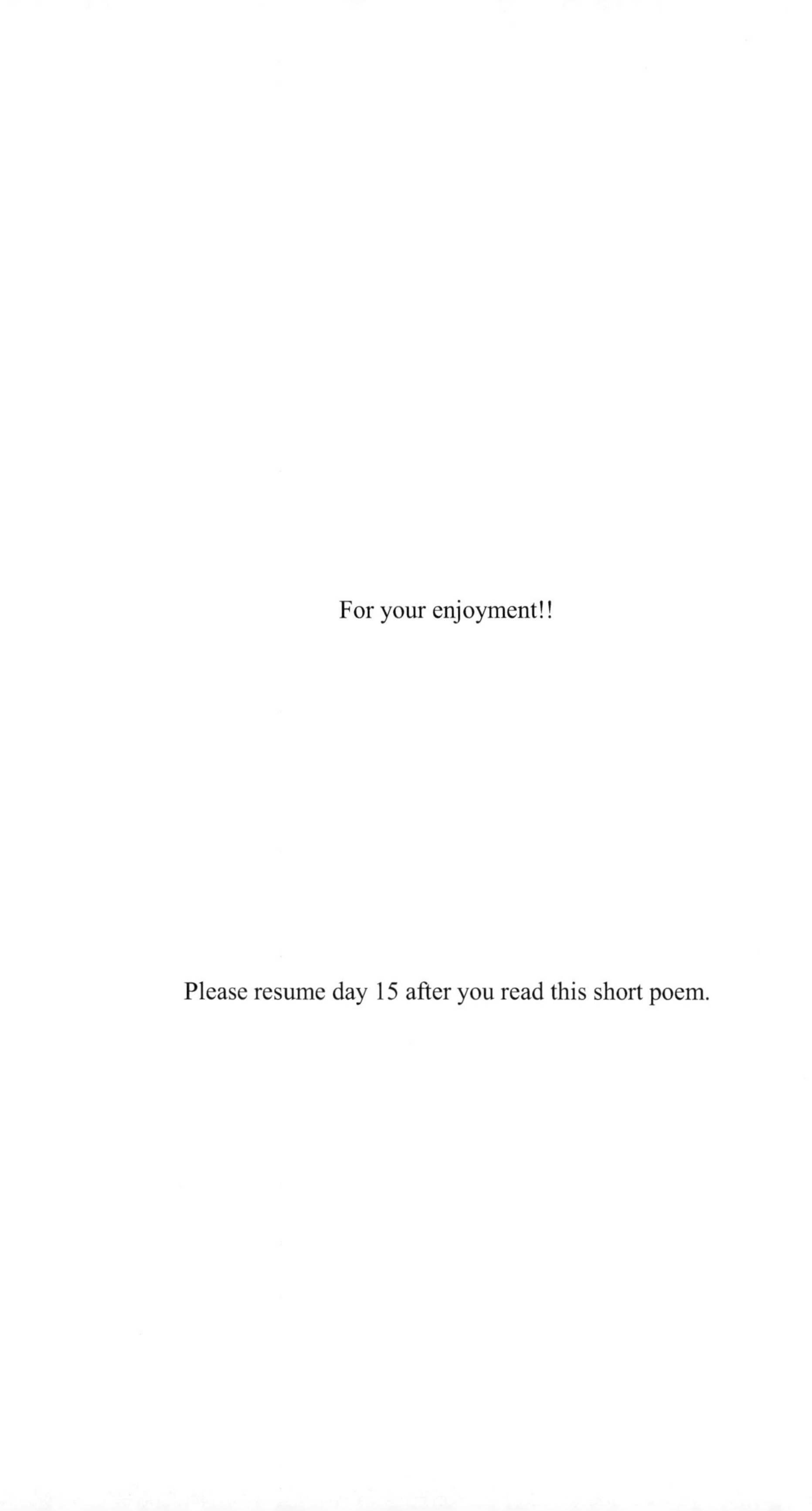

For your enjoyment!!

Please resume day 15 after you read this short poem.

A Knight in Dull Armor

So you're a Knight in shining armor,
a mighty man of valor;
women swoon, crowds croon
and demons fear your power.
You walk through towns with head held high,
a prince in all his glory;
but deep inside you've got no pride,
you know the real story.
At the end of the day when the crowds go away
you retreat to sit and think;
and to polish your armor to a perfect spit shine,
"Wait! Is that a chink?"
You run you finger over the break,
a definite indention.
You search every inch of your entire suit
with a strong and fervent intention.
There's a scratch, and there's a dent
and there's another too.
How could you not see all these imperfections
that cover the whole of you?
You've worked so hard to stay rust-free
and shine it every night.
The demons have no power over you
they cower at your very sight.
Their weapons are useless and just for show;
they're all just smoke and mirrors.
The only thing they have on you
is playing on your fears.
But that doesn't work and hasn't for years,
for as far back as you can think.
But if that's true, and you know it is,
Where did you get that chink?
If these dents and scratches didn't come from out there,
they must have come from within.
Bad decisions and little compromises,
It's your integrity that has done you in.
That time you stole, that time you lied
and especially that time you cheated;
no enemy could touch you
but by yourself you were defeated.
It was wrong to do it, you know that now
but these dents wont go away.
You clean and scrub, polish and shine
but they are here to stay.

A Damsel, But Not in Distress

So you're an independent woman, a beautiful lady,
a damsel, but not in distress.
You control your world, every single inch,
all while wearing heels and a dress.
There's nothing you need, and anything you want
you'll go out and get it yourself.
You've made your way and ran your race,
won trophies to put on your shelf.
But when somebody hints that you may be wrong
and they bring up that word "submission,"
you politely grin and lift up your chin,
for you know your marital position.
You love your husband and know he loves you
but sometimes he has no precision.
You can get it done faster all by yourself,
besides, he makes bad decisions.
You try to ignore that voice deep down inside,
and take pride in keeping things tight.
You're lonely and sad, he gets quiet when he's mad,
but you're not a damsel in distress, right?
You were crafted, you see, by a loving Creator
with a plan for your very life.
He chose you specifically for this wonderful man
who loves you and made you his wife.
Neither his mom nor his maid, not his leader or boss,
you're not designed to fulfill that role.
You were designed as his helper, for him to protect,
being rescued actually fulfills your soul.
"So you're supposed to submit and just do what he says,"
as if that would make your marriage great.
But slavery is wrong and should never be used,
"You should be equals with your mate."
Perhaps you misunderstand what submission really is.
God never placed you under your husband's thumb.
You're there as his queen, the love of his life,
not lesser, not stupid, not dumb.
God designed your husband for blessings and success,
but only with you by his side.
You're the only woman in this entire world
that can make this man swell up with pride.
He lives for your smile and strives for your pleasure
but shuts down when he can't please his bride.
Submission, you see, is not being a slave
but rather making your husband come alive.

A Knight in Dull Armor---continued.

The crowds will see and be disappointed
at the lack of reflection on your steel.
It will be so hard to impress them now
with imperfections that are very real.
Should you just go on and walk around
as a knight in old dull armor?
You wish you could quit and take up a trade
as a butcher, a baker or a farmer?
But a knight you are and that won't stop
even if you change your vocation;
and your integrity follows you anyway,
no matter your location.
So stand up high and wear it with pride,
this suit of dents and dings.
Don't worry about what the crowd sees,
they don't know everything.
They don't know how and they don't know why,
they don't know what these dents are.
They won't understand, without a war
how you got these battle scars.
Yes, you've failed, you've made mistakes
you've fallen, you must confess.
But you got back up and learned your lesson
and now you fall down even less.
Yes they're there and visible
for everyone to see;
but they are not who you are today,
they're who you used to be.
They are a true picture, a story if you will,
that you can be proud of;
a story of hope, a story of forgiveness,
an incredible story of love.
You fight for a King who sees everything
and loves you anyway.
He knows what you did and He is quick to forgive
and He washes the filth away.
The crowd still sees a fantastic knight
in armor that is glowing.
It's because you are a reflection of Him,
it's His glory that you are showing.
So wear your chinks proudly and don't be ashamed,
they are what you have overcome.
It's all just a part of being a knight
and fighting with the Son!

A Damsel, But Not in Distress---continued.

Being his queen and making him king
doesn't mean you are less or lower than.
To fully achieve what you were created to be
you must embrace the way God set the plan.
You're the daughter of God, His most precious creation,
and He chose a fantastic blessing for you;
His favorite son, to be your husband,
to be loving and protecting and true.
Submitting to your man doesn't hold you back,
it actually frees you to escape the mess.
And it totally creates a conquering hero
who was designed for a damsel in distress.
Your husband is a warrior, a mighty man of valor
and he is designed to want one woman's respect.
With your love and support and encouragement,
he'll do more than either of you expect.
God set this system up for you both to succeed
when your man is respected by a specific one.
Without your respect and love, the respect of others
is as good as the respect of none.
Your gentle submission is the key to this thing.
Your respect will cause more of his love.
Don't believe me? Try it and see.
Watch your marriage be blessed from above.
There's nothing wrong with you or the way God made you,
You are loved and cherished and blessed.
And it would bless your husband if you could step back
and let him rescue his damsel in distress.

Day 15
Shining Your Armor

You are her knight in shining armor. You are a chivalrous and strong, confident warrior that looks so good standing guard over her. Every little thing you do to protect, honor, cherish, and love her simply puts a new shine to your suit of armor.

But if you are reading this book, whether it was your idea or hers, it is probably because that suit of armor needs a little polish. It may look shiny to you from the inside, but you are not the one who is supposed to be impressed by the shine...she is.

It's time to get that armor so shiny that your beautiful bride would be honored to be rescued by you. This is actually not that hard. I can give you a list of things to do like opening her door for her and washing her car. You can leave her love notes and clean the house and even send her flowers. The problem is that you have tried all of this before, with no effect. Why didn't it work?

Checking off boxes on a list is just that. You will never break through the wall she has built by doing that. You have to love her with all your heart before these little acts mean anything. Even then, it is going to take time for her to see that your love is real.

STOP TRYING TO WIN SOMETHING AND LOVE HER FOR HER SAKE!

There are no shortcuts. You have to be willing to go to battle for her love and we rarely know ahead of time how long the battle will last. If you are willing to show her your love, over and over again, with no end in sight, you will have your victory. She will begin to see your true love and respond to it. Keep shining your armor with little instances of romance and love, and keep loving her deeply, without looking for the reward and eventually she will believe that you truly love her.

Love never fails. 1 Corinthians 13:8 (NIV)

You can often get hints from her as to ways to make your armor shine brighter. Listen for clues in what she says and thinks. What thrills her heart? What kind of shows does she like to watch? What are the little things that she has to do that you could do for her? All these things are like adding extra polish to your suit and will all work in your favor once she is able to see your love.

Day 15
Damsel in Distress

I'm not sure "Distress" is quite the right word. I'm not even sure you would like to be called a "Damsel." You probably don't even need rescuing.

But you have a Knight in Shining Armor looking for a chance to rescue you. Okay, maybe his armor isn't that shiny and maybe he doesn't appear to be much of a knight, and maybe he doesn't seem to be trying to rescue you, but that doesn't matter because you are not a Damsel in Distress...right?

Unless you feel like life is hard. Maybe you feel the stress of work, family, friends and even the stress of feeling like you are not walking close enough to God. Maybe you are under attack. The enemy has worked hard to separate you from God, friends, family and especially from your knight.

The hurts that you have experienced are very real, but they have become the bricks in the wall around you. The enemy has been investing heavily in the construction of this wall and he has helped you build this wall high, long, deep and extremely thick. The more separated you are from your wonderful husband, the easier it is for the enemy to tell you lies about him. The enemy convinces you that your loving husband isn't so loving and that your chivalrous knight is more concerned about himself that he is about you. He convinces you that you are not loved. He beats you down with examples of your husband's failures, experiences and constantly repeats the harsh words your knight has spoken in the past. You feel trapped.

There is a way out! Allow yourself to be rescued!

Needing to be rescued doesn't mean you are weak, frail or even a failure any more that needing Christ as a Savior makes you less of God's most precious child. The fact is that you were designed to be rescued.

Then they cried out to the LORD in their trouble; He saved them out of their distresses. Psalm 107:19 (NIV)

You were designed by God to need your Knight...and he was designed to learn how to rescue you with his love. As he fights for you and beats back the enemy's forces to free you from that bondage, your loving husband becomes more of the man God created him to be. He needs to learn to fight for you, he needs to learn to love you and he needs you to believe in him. Show him how to bless you. Show him how to please you. Show him how to rescue his wife, his love, his damsel in distress.

The more you let him rescue you, the more his armor will shine and the more he will become that chivalrous Knight releasing you from the enemy's grip. Then you will let him recue you just because it is fun!

Day 15

Dear Lord,

I come to you tonight and thank you that you have chosen me to be the one to rescue your daughter. Thank you for teaching me how to reach her and how to impress her.

Lord I ask that you help me continue to impress her and show her how much I care for her. I ask you Lord to help me keep a shine on my armor that my beautiful wife will always be able to see. Help me to know the little things that will impress my gorgeous bride.

Help me Lord to strive to impress her with my life. I know as you lead me, she will see that I am yours and begin to trust me as she trusts you. Help me be the knight that she is excited about. Help me be the man that she is so impressed with.

Lord I ask you to help me to continually shine my armor for my amazing queen that you have given me. Don't ever let me stop trying to bless her and take care of her as you have anointed me to do. Lord, bless her with the ability to see the gestures and hear the words I say that bless her and help my beautiful bride allow me to be her knight in shining armor.

Lord, we stand together tonight and ask for your healing hand on our marriage. We resist the enemy and command him to leave as we submit our lives, our home and our marriage to You.

We stand, praying this in the name of Your Son, Jesus Christ, our Lord; Amen.

Day 15

Dear Lord,

I come to you tonight and thank you for creating me to love and be loved. Thank you for rescuing me from hell and into eternal life with You.

Thank you for a mighty man that you have given to me to rescue me and keep me safe in this harsh, hurtful world.

Lord I ask you to help me show him how to reach me. Help me lead him into loving me and protecting me. Help me to love and respect him as he learns how to rescue me.

Lord I ask you to help me show him how wonderful he truly is and how much I want to be rescued by him. Help me to trust him as he fights for me, even when I don't see him fighting. Help me to trust You in him as You lead him to win my heart each and every day.

Lord, help me to be the damsel that he is looking for. Show me how to impress him and please him. Show me how to be beautiful for him and let him see the beauty You created, even when I don't feel beautiful.

Lord, help me pray and fight for my Knight as he fights for me. Help me to always look for the best in him even as the enemy is telling me lies about him. Help me to find ways to bless my wonderful husband with my love.

Day 16
Safe and Secure

You must know by now that your wonderful wife sees all of your mistakes. She knows where you fail, where you fall short and even where you just give up. She is the closest one to you and she sees it all. Think about it...it has got to be difficult for her to know that God told her to follow you and watch you fail, over and over. It must be tough for her to continue to follow someone that is was failing, falling and giving up...unless she knows that you are being mentored by Somebody much greater than yourself.

As your beautiful bride sees you fail, she needs to see that you are being led by God. She needs to have confidence that you can handle this because He can handle this. She needs to feel safe and secure.

If you are willing to be vulnerable and show her that you do not have all the answers, but you know that God does, then she can feel safe in you because she will understand that you are operating in God's protection and blessing.

As His children, we are all secure in His love. We have the surety of going to Heaven as well as being blessed while we are here on earth. However, we often operate our lives based upon our feelings. These feelings may line up with the truth or they may be completely invalid...but they are still the way we feel.

Your beautiful bride is no exception. She has feelings about the future. She has feelings about you and your leading. Whether they are accurate or not is irrelevant at this point...you have to deal with them. Assure her that she can rest in God's security the same way that you do.

Whoever dwells in the shelter of the Most High will rest in the shadow of the Almighty. Psalm 91:1 (NIV)

Many times her comfort will come from God through you. Her safety will come from God through you. Her security will come from God through you. As you show her that you are weak and depend on God, she will see you as strong enough to depend on Him and therefore be able to depend on you.

As you show your beautiful bride that you do not have all the answers, but you depend on God, and know that He will never leave you or forsake you, she will be safe and secure putting her trust in you as her leader.

You are a great leader because you are following God.

Day 16
Admiration and Support

You see all of his mistakes. You watch him as he fails... over and over.

Your incredible husband is always going to make mistakes, just like you will. But he has a unique desire placed deep within him that causes him to seek out, strive for and sometimes even ask for your approval.

He has the daunting task of leading you in an area that he has never been before and he knows that he is accountable to God for you. You are his most precious treasure and he was completely thrilled when he won your heart in marriage...even if he didn't show it. God designed your amazing husband to spend his life trying to impress one very special woman...you.

And now he knows that he keeps falling short and making mistakes in front of you, and the embarrassment and shame are manifesting itself in pride and anger. He could handle failing in front of just about everybody...except you.

He wants you to be impressed. He wants you to be totally smitten with him. He would love it if you could ignore the fact that you just saw him fail and act like he is just the perfect specimen of a man.

And you can! You can totally trust your mighty man of God knowing that he is learning how to follow God. In reality, you know that you can trust God in your husband. God will never fail you.

Wives, understand and support your husbands in ways that show your support for Christ. Ephesians 5:22 (MSG)

Your Godly support and admiration of your loving husband will continue to feed the Godly characteristics that you genuinely admire in him. It is a beautiful cyclical design in which the more you bless your husband in words and actions, the more he becomes the man that God has called him to be...the man you want him to be.

Your wonderful husband will learn more of the loving heart of God and how He is the lifter of his head through you and your admiration and support in the midst of his failings. He will be able to see the softer side of God as you show him love and respect at times that he is expecting harsh rebukes and criticism.

Deal with him the way Jesus deals with you, never holding his sin against him. It is not your gifting, your calling or even your responsibility to convict him. That is the job of the Holy Spirit and you can have complete confidence that He will do it right.

You, however are designed by God to help your loving husband hear the Holy Spirit speaking to him. This is best done by your quiet, gentle submission...i.e. your support and admiration.

Day 16

Dear Lord,

I come to you tonight and thank you for the safety and security that you give to me. I know that I am your child and that you keep me under your wing. I know that you go to battle for me and are my shield and the rock that I stand upon.

Lord, I ask that you help me be strong enough to admit my weaknesses to you. Help me to yield to you and simply accept the wonderful victory that you have.

Lord, I thank you for the precious gift of my wife.

Lord, I ask you to help me be vulnerable in front of the wonderful woman that you gave me. Help me to show her that I depend on You. Help me to lead her in feeling safe and secure in You through me. Help me to strengthen her in her feelings about You as I grow stronger in my feelings for You because of Your truth.

Lord, I ask You to help me not be led by my feelings, but by your word. Help me to form my feelings from your truth that you say about me and my beautiful bride.

Lord I ask You to strengthen my relationship with my wonderful wife. I ask you to help us depend on You through each other and I ask you to help her feel safe and secure in spite of seeing my faults and failings.

Lord, we stand together tonight and ask for your healing hand on our marriage. We resist the enemy and command him to leave as we submit our lives, our home and our marriage to You.

We stand, praying this in the name of Your Son, Jesus Christ, our Lord; Amen.

Day 16

Dear Lord,

I come to you tonight and thank you for the safety and security that you give to me. I know that I am your child and that you keep me under your wing. I know that you go to battle for me and are my shield and the rock that I stand upon.

Lord, I ask you to help me not be led by my feelings, but by your word. Help me to form my feelings from your truth that you say about me and my loving husband.

Lord, I thank you for the gift of my loving husband. I thank you that he strives to follow after you. Help me to constantly lift him up in prayer to you.

Lord, I ask that you help me be the supportive woman that builds my wonderful husband up. Help me to see him more and more the way that you see him.

I ask you Lord to help me focus on his blessings and achievements and not on his failures. Help me to give you complete control over pointing out his shortcomings and his faults.

Lord, help him to be able to be vulnerable in front of me and help me to be a blessing to him as his encourager and supporter.

Show my wonderful husband that he can be even stronger in You by admitting his weaknesses to you. Help him yield to you and accept your victory as his own.

Lord I ask you to help me to strengthen and empower him with my love and support.

Lord I ask you to strengthen my relationship with my loving husband. I ask you to help us depend on You through each other and I ask you to help him to know that he is a great leader in spite of all of his faults and failings.

Day 17
Treat Her Like a Lady

It's not just how you speak to her and it's not just opening doors for her. Treating your wonderful wife like a lady is actually a very spiritual thing.

Your bride is a treasure and still highly valued by the One who gave her to you. She is God's princess and when He gave her to you, He expected you to treat her as such.

With a large segment of society clamoring for individuality and independence, it is easy to get distracted from what it is that we truly desire and what it is that we truly need...value. Your beautiful bride is trying to avoid what the world says but it is a struggle because she doesn't believe what God says about her.

The world says that she is one of the masses.

God says that she is unique and created exactly the way He wants her.

The world says that she is not loved, but nobody is loved, so it is okay.

God says that she is valued above everything and He died for her.

Your beautiful bride needs to feel her value and she is designed by her loving creator to derive that value from Him through you. When she cannot determine her value from her husband, she will allow the rest of the world to decide her value. Over time, she will forget how to go about getting her value from God through you, but her true, innate value is still there, waiting to be discovered, revealed, and shown off to the world.

And let the beauty of the Lord our God be upon us. And establish the work of our hands for us; Psalm 90:17 (NKJV)

All of the external things that you do, opening doors and waiting on her hand and foot are symbolic gestures that show that you do value her. They show her, they show the world, they show yourself and most of all they show her heavenly Father that you hold her in high esteem and showing God that you value her is like bowing to His royalty. As you treat her like a lady, God will renew in her the desire to be your lady. He will faithfully bring her heart back to the one who was designed to love her, to honor her and to treat her like a lady...you.

Treat her like a lady and you will bring out the passionate, loving and gorgeous lady that God created for you.

Show your beautiful bride how valuable she is and she will show you how valuable you are.

Day 17
Treat Him Like a Man

It's not about him watching football on Sunday. It's not about him needing to go out with the boys. And it's definitely not about him being stronger than you. Treating your husband like a man is actually a very spiritual thing.

Your man is actually a mighty man of God. He is a son and is deemed as royalty. You have been specifically chosen by God, the designer of this great marriage, to make this man into the son he is supposed to be. It is a daunting task, but you are more than up to it. God created you to be. You and only you are the one who can draw out of your husband the greatness that God has put in him.

This world is yelling at him to be what they want him to be. They want him more feminine or more masculine. They want him more tolerant and less godly. They want him to be theirs. Your wonderful husband struggles to avoid hearing them because he doesn't believe what God says about him.

But he is God's son and God has designed you to show him how to be a man of God.

Be good wives to your husbands, responsive to their needs. ...indifferent as they are to any words about God, (they) will be captivated by your life of holy beauty. 1 Peter 3:1 (MSG)

By loving him deeply, your husband begins to see God's love even more. By believing in him, your loving man becomes someone who can be believed. By trusting him, your mighty man becomes trustworthy.

You see, God designed man to need a helper. It is not a lowly position, it is a power position. You have the power to make this man into whatever you can believe. He is designed to become the man that you believe for. He is designed by a loving creator to derive his value from God through you. Your husband, your lover, your amazing, kind, thoughtful, trustworthy, caring man is that way because you choose to believe the Holy Spirit that is within him.

When you see him trip, fall and fail; just keep believing the truth that God tells you about him. He is a good man. He is a loving man. He is a gentle, God-fearing man of integrity. The more you speak it, the more you will believe it. The more you believe it, the more it will be true of your incredible husband.

Treat him like a man and you will bring out the tender but powerful, soft but strong, fierce but loving leader that God calls him to be for you.

Day 17

Dear Lord,

I come to you tonight and thank you for treating me as your son. Thank you for your patience and kindness toward me even when I make mistakes. Thank you for creating me to be more than a conqueror and treating me as such.

I ask you to forgive me for not treating my beautiful wife as well as I should. I ask you to help me treat her like the lady that you created her to be. Help me treat her, the way that You do and help me to recognize when I am not treating her like a lady.

Lord, help her to forgive me for not treating her as well as I should. Help her to release anything she is holding against me and help her to see my heart and my desire to treat her well.

Lord, help me to understand more and more how to treat my wonderful wife and how to take care of her in everything I do.

Lord, we stand together tonight and ask for your healing hand on our marriage. We resist the enemy and command him to leave as we submit our lives, our home and our marriage to You.

We stand, praying this in the name of Your Son, Jesus Christ, our Lord; Amen.

Day 17

Dear Lord,

I come to you tonight and thank you for treating me as a lady. Thank you for your patience and kindness toward me even when I make mistakes. Thank you for creating me to be more than a conqueror and treating me as such.

I ask you to forgive me for not treating my wonderful husband as well as I should. I ask you to help me treat him like the man of God that you created him to be. Help me treat him the way that You do and help me to recognize when I am not treating him like a man.

Lord, help him to forgive me for not treating him as well as I should. Help him to release anything he is holding against me and help him to see my heart and my desire to treat him well.

Lord, help me to understand more and more how to treat my wonderful husband and how to take care of his heart in everything I do.

Day 18
Role of a Counselor

Just as you have been commissioned to lead your family, your amazing bride has a mantle of leadership placed upon her as well. It is very important that you recognize the blessing that God has given you in providing her with the insight and wisdom that she has. She has been uniquely blessed for one main task...to help you.

God knew everything that you would need to accomplish your task of winning the heart of His beautiful princess and He has provided it all. But much of what you need, and much of what you need to learn will come from the princess herself...your beautiful bride.

God has designed your relationship with her and with Him to be ultimately achieved when you fit into the pattern that He designed for your life. This pattern is actually created around your lovely wife. She will have insight from God in areas that she may not even realize. She will have wisdom that you need to advance your life, your relationships and even your spiritual connection to God.

Remember, God gave you the task of leading her to Him, and the closer she gets to you, the closer she can get to Him. And God did not place her here to distract you from Him, but to draw you closer to Him. He will use her to teach you, lead you, help you and bless you. She is designed by God for you. She has your same vision and goals already planted in her and it fulfills her to be a part of what God is doing in you.

You may often find yourself rejecting her counsel, thinking that you are the one that is supposed to know best. Understand this...

The way of fools seems right to them, but the wise listen to advice. Proverbs 12:15

...and your beautiful bride is actually a very wise woman and should always be your main source of counsel. Just like you are specifically designed by God to lead this family, your incredibly beautiful wife is designed to be more than just eye-candy for you. She is full of wisdom that God wants you to have; but you can only get it through her. Your submission to her counsel is a huge part of the way God designed this relationship to work. Listen to your wonderful wife and learn how best to lead her and love her; and how to be incredibly successful in life.

Day 18
Role of a Leader

Your wonderful husband has a job to do. He is to be the leader of your family...sounds easy enough. But let's look at what is really being asked of him.

The Creator of the Universe has called upon your loving husband to be in charge and therefore accountable for your children, your home, your ministry, your successes, your failures and most importantly....you.

Just imagine for a second being responsible to lead someone to a place, in a direction, in a way that you have never been before. Sure, it is quite possible, but then you feel the pressure of accountability. You know that one day, possibly everyday, you must face your king and give an account for how you did, what you did, and why you did it. You have to stand before the almighty God and tell Him why you didn't follow His leading; why you acted out in anger, why you failed. The real problem is that you feel deep down inside you that you are not qualified to do this. You feel like a failure faking your way through life. This world says that married couples can share the responsibility, but you know deep inside that you have been given full, accountable responsibility for what happens here.

This is the position that your loving husband is in everyday. He may handle it very well, he may pretend as though he has everything under control, or he may not even know why he is so stressed. But, you now know how to help, how to encourage and most of all how to pray for him.

Therefore encourage one another and build each other up, just as in fact you are doing. 1 Thessalonians 5:11 (NIV)

He will be looking to you for counsel because he knows God has put you here as his chief counselor. He will be looking for clues on how to lead you and how to bless you, but he may not want you to know that he is leaning on you. He wants you to be impressed with his leadership abilities. He wants you to be impressed with him.

Just the right look or words of affirmation from you can propel him into confidence in his leadership. He needs to know that you believe in him. He needs to know that you think he is a good leader. He needs to know that you believe that God did not make a mistake when He chose your husband for you.

Affirm, support and stand behind your leader as you craft, mold and shape him into what God has called him to be...a Mighty Man of God and Your Blessed Husband.

Day 18

Dear Lord,

I come to you tonight and thank you for the opportunity to lead my family. I thank you for blessing me with such a wonderful wife to be by my side.

Lord I ask you to forgive me for the times that I have rejected your counsel through her. I ask you to help me recognize everyday that she is such a wise woman of God and that you designed her to work with me and not against me. Forgive me for all the times that I have been proud and tried to do things on my own.

Lord, help me to see my beautiful bride as the wonderful counselor that she is. Help me to make her a part of everything that you are doing in me. Help me to make her my chief counsel in all things as I know you have placed her here to bless me and not to hold me back in any way.

Show her that I truly do recognize the gifts that you have placed on her and that those incredibly valuable traits are not just for her but for the advancement of our family, our marriage and our relationship.

Bless her with even more wisdom and allow me to learn, grow and prosper because You have given her to me to be my helpmate, my lover and my queen. Help me to understand more and more as you guide me in wisdom through my beautiful bride.

Lord, we stand together tonight and ask for your healing hand on our marriage. We resist the enemy and command him to leave as we submit our lives, our home and our marriage to You.

We stand, praying this in the name of Your Son, Jesus Christ, our Lord; Amen.

Day 18

Dear Lord,

I come to you tonight and thank you for the husband you gave me to lead my family. I thank you for blessing me with such a wonderful man of God for me to stand by.

Lord I ask you to forgive me for the times that I have rejected your leadership through him. I ask you to help me recognize everyday that he is such a wise man of God and that you designed him to lead and bless me; not to control or hinder me.

Lord, help me to see my amazing husband as the wonderful leader that he is. Help me to recognize that he is a part of everything that you are doing in me.

Show him that I truly do recognize the gifts that you have placed on him. Show him that I believe in him as I believe in you. Show him that He is the perfect man to lead me. Help me show him how much I love and admire him.

Bless him with even more wisdom and allow me to learn, grow and prosper because You have given him to me to be my leader, my lover and my king. Help me to understand more and more as you guide me in wisdom through my incredible husband.

Day 19
Love and Respect

You are commanded to love your wife. Simple...Done...Next subject.

However, each one of you also must love his wife as he loves himself, Ephesians 5:33 (NIV)

Not so fast. How can you be commanded by God in Ephesians to produce an emotion? How can God order you to feel a certain way? Actually...He didn't. We have been conditioned to believe that love is an emotion...it is not. Love is an action and you have the ability to make the decision to love.

You are to love your beautiful bride the way Christ loves the church...His people...you! You are to lay down your life for His princess that He has entrusted to you and you are to love her with all your heart.

God has commanded her in the same chapter to respect you. Respect is an action and she has the ability to make the decision to respect. These actions will bring about emotions in each of you but these actions themselves are not emotions. As you love her she will feel love. As she respects you, you will feel respected. Both of these actions are simple...not easy! It might be easier for you to respect somebody.. And it seems that love comes easier to women. Why is God asking you to do something that is so against your natural feel?

The truth is that God created you to feel real love from one woman, but you feel it through the level of respect that she has for you. In the same way, God created your beautiful wife to want, need and feel real love from one man...you. She is blessed, inspired and encouraged to become all that God has created her to be by the feeling that she gets through your love. So God put it in you to love her, but He couldn't make it automatic or it wouldn't be genuine and it has to be genuinely yours.

And God couldn't make it based on how you feel because those feeling would be based on your bride's performance and God never, ever bases His love on our performance. He loves us no matter what.

It is going to be hard for you to love her when you do not feel respected by her. Love her anyway; You are empowered through grace to do it.

In the same way, it is going to be hard for her to respect you when she doesn't feel love from you. She is commanded to respect you by God and that is between her and God...He will deal with that. Your job is to love her and show her love and then love her some more. Love her with your life and your whole heart. The more you love her, the more you will break through the wall that has been built between you and she will begin to see, feel and enjoy your love.

You have one job...Love your beautiful bride.

Day 19
Love and Respect

Your husband is commanded by God in Ephesians to Love you...and yet, so many times, you don't feel loved.

You, on the other hand are commanded in the same text to respect your husband. How can God tell you to feel respect? How can God command you to feel an emotion?

Actually...He didn't. This world has conditioned us to believe that both love and respect are emotions that we can turn on and off. The truth of it is that while there are definitely the emotional aspects of love and respect, these are not feelings, they are decisions, and you are fully capable of making these decisions in spite of your feelings.

...each one of you also must love his wife as he loves himself, and the wife must respect her husband. Ephesians 5:33 (NIV)

God commands you to respect your husband whether he is worthy of it or not. This is actually easier said than done as I am sure you have figured out.

It seems that loving people comes easier to women and respecting people might come easier to men. Why is God asking you to do something that is so against your grain? The truth is that God created you to feel real love from one man and to be empowered by that feeling. In the same way, God created your wonderful husband to look for, long for, even strive for the respect of one woman...you. He is encouraged, inspired and empowered to become the mighty man of God by the feeling he gets when he has your respect. So God put it in you to respect him. But God couldn't make it automatic or it would not be genuine...and it has to be genuinely yours. And God couldn't make it based on your feelings or those would be based on your husbands performance and God doesn't ever rate us on performance...He loves us no matter what.

No, God told you to see to it that you respect him and the more you do, the more you will begin to feel the respect for your incredible husband. And the more you feel respect for him, the more he will feel that respect and will become the loving husband that you so desire and he will treat you with love. Your respect teaches him how to love. He is commanded by God to love you and if he isn't doing it well, the Holy Spirit will be sure to deal with him. You just continue to respect him and create an atmosphere for him to feel your respect and begin to love you the way you should be loved...like a queen.

Love your husband by respecting him, and you have this promise...***Love never fails. 1 Corinthians 13:8 (NIV)***

Day 19

Dear Lord,

I come to You tonight and thank You for loving me. I thank You Lord, for being my example of how to love my wonderful wife.

Lord, I ask You tonight to teach me how to love. Teach me more about how You love me and how I can love the lady that You gave me with all my heart. Help me show her love in every way that I can. Help me to lay my life down for her the way You laid heaven aside to come to earth for me.

Lord I ask You to help me make my beautiful bride feel my love. I ask You to give me the right words to say at the right time that will make her feel love. I ask You to give me witty ideas of how to show her my love and how to express love to her more and more.

I ask You Lord to help me continue to make the decision to love her when I have had a hard day or may not feel like it. Help me to understand that love is not an emotion but a decision and I decide right now that I love my wife with all my heart. Help me to never base my love for her on any conditions or emotions.

Lord, I ask You to help her see my love even as I am unskilled at showing and telling her. Give her grace to feel my love as I learn more and more how to love her the way You love me.

Lord, we stand together tonight and ask for Your healing hand on our marriage. We resist the enemy and command him to leave as we submit our lives, our home and our marriage to You.

We stand, praying this in the name of Your Son, Jesus Christ, our Lord; Amen.

Day 19

Dear Lord,

I come to You tonight and thank You for loving me. I thank You Lord, for being my example of how to respect my incredible husband.

Lord, I ask You tonight to teach me how to show love to my wonderful husband by respecting him. Teach me more about how You love me and how I can love the incredible man that You gave me with all my heart. Help me show him love and respect in every way that I can. Help me to lay my life down for him the way You laid heaven aside to come to earth for me.

Lord I ask You to help me make my wonderful husband feel my respect. I ask You to give me the right words to say at the right time that will make him feel loved and respected. I ask You to give me great ideas of how to show him my respect and how to express my love to him more and more.

I ask You Lord to help me continue to make the decision to respect him when I have had a hard day or even when I may not feel like it. Help me to understand that respect is not an emotion but a decision and I decide right now that I love my husband with all my heart and I do respect him. Help me to never base my love and respect for him on any conditions or emotions.

Lord, I ask You to help him see my love even as I am unskilled at showing and telling him. Give him grace to feel respect from me as I learn more and more how to love him the way You love me.

Day 20
Saving the Best for Last

Your beautiful bride is always going to be your number one source of counsel, support and encouragement...and yet she is usually the one who gets the "left-overs" of your day.

Shortly after you were wed to the most amazing woman you had ever met, it became very easy to focus on what is next in life. Work, friends, building assets, and even vacationing became more important than putting your wonderful wife first. It is a very normal occurrence. You didn't even mean to demote her on the priority list and you may not even believe that she is less of a priority, but your marriage says otherwise...doesn't it?

The truth is that we take each other for granted simply because we can. We are together all the time and once she has seen your imperfections, there is no need to hide them any longer. So you don't. It's a lot of work to continue to try to impress her by doing things that are not required. And she will readily admit that she is "fine" with the way it is. She says that stuff doesn't even bother her. But you know deep down that you could be doing this better. You know that you are not giving her the best of you. After all, you have to put on a good front for friends, co-workers, church and other family. You and she are on the same team and have the same goals and vision, so you should be able to let your guard down around your wife...right?

Yes, you should be able to. But that doesn't mean that she shouldn't be the one you strive to impress above all others. She should be the one that you save the good stuff for. She should be the one that you work hardest to impress, dress nicest for and pay attention to the most. Your marriage will outlast relationships with other family, friends and even outlast your employer. You are in this for the long run; let's impress the one who is in this with you for the long run...your beautiful bride.

Consider how far you have fallen! Repent and do the things you did at first. Revelation 2:5 (NIV)

As you strive to impress her, your wonderful wife will feel your love acted out towards her. She will begin to see that you don't just love her because you are "commanded to by God," but that you genuinely like her. She will know that after all that you had to do in your day; you saved the best for last...for her.

Day 20
Saving the Best for Last

You have an amazing husband that loves you more than anyone else on earth. He thinks about you all the time and longs to be with you. He knows your deepest hurts and your highest joys...and yet he is the one who usually gets the "left-overs" of your day.

After you were wed to the most incredible man you had ever met, after the dating was over and after the honeymoon, it became very easy to begin focusing on the next project in life. You try to be excited to see him at the end of your hard day but little by little, life begins to take more and more energy. So many things became urgent issues to handle and before you knew it, your wonderful lover became just a real good friend.

He is operating in the same world and under the same conditions so he completely understands. Neither of you are upset with the other, and you even discuss this being a temporary situation that will fix itself once our family is stable financially.

The truth is that we take each other for granted just because we can. We have seen each others imperfections and now there is no reason to hide them...so you don't. It is actually a lot of work to continue to try to impress someone who already knows everything about you. He has stopped trying to impress you too, and even told you that he is fine with the way it is. He loves you just the way you are. He truly does and you love him, but you know deep down that you are not giving the love of your life, your best.

You should be able to be real and let your guard down around your wonderful husband without it lessening the romance between you. He wants to live with passion just as you do. But being able to relax around your loving husband doesn't mean that you shouldn't strive to impress him. He should be the one on your mind as you choose your outfit for the day. He should be the one that you pay attention to the most; the one you smile for, the one you compliment and the one that has your eye as well as your heart.

Consider how far you have fallen! Repent and do the things you did at first. Revelation 2:5 (NIV)

As you strive to impress him, your amazing husband will begin to feel the love that you are acting out towards him. He will begin to realize that you don't just love him...you like him. He will be attracted to the passion you have for him and realize that after all that you had to do in your day, you saved the best of yourself for last...for him.

Day 20

Dear Lord,

I come to You tonight and thank You for Your love and Your life. Thank You that after all that You had to give, You saved your best for me. You gave up heaven to come and save me. Thank You for always giving me Your best.

Lord I ask You to forgive me for not making your princess my priority. I recognize that You gave her to me to love, honor and cherish and I want to hold her as a priority in my life. I want to truly show her that I love her.

Lord, I ask You to help me give my best to my beautiful bride. Help me to focus on impressing her more than impressing others. Help me to remember how important she is and to always put her first as my priority. Help me reserve the best of myself for her at the end of the day. Help me to show her that I put her first and that I do intentionally make her my priority.

Lord, we stand together tonight and ask for Your healing hand on our marriage. We resist the enemy and command him to leave as we submit our lives, our home and our marriage to You.

We stand, praying this in the name of Your Son, Jesus Christ, our Lord; Amen.

Day 20

Dear Lord,

I come to You tonight and thank You for Your love and Your life. Thank You that after all that You had to give, You saved Your best for me. You gave up heaven to come and save me. Thank You for always giving me Your best.

Lord I ask You to forgive me for not making my husband my priority. I recognize that You gave him to me to love, honor and respect and I want to love and respect him the way I did when we were first in love.

Lord, I ask You to help me give my best to my wonderful husband. Help me to focus on impressing him more than impressing others. Help me to remember how important he is and to always put him first as my priority. Help me reserve the best of myself for him at the end of the day. Help me to show him that I put him first and that I do intentionally make him my priority.

Day 21
Let Her See You

You are a strong leader, a victorious warrior and more than a conqueror. That is why God has chosen you for this leadership position. You are the right man for the job and it is because God created you to be that man.

But you have a gentle side too...not a weak side, a gentle side. You have compassion for those that are hurting. You care about people that are suffering. You are a very loving man that wants to show love to people. You actually have feelings and when you are not trying to hide them, and when you are not trying to describe them, they show. You are a very emotional creation. You don't want anybody to see this because you think it may make you appear to be weak. But you are not weak.

Your wonderful wife needs to see these traits. These characteristics were placed in you by God. He has created you to accomplish greater works than He did when He was on earth and you can only do that if you are operating in the gifts that He gave you. Your beautiful bride has these characteristics as well, but we tend to think of emotions as fitting for a woman. They are part of God's character and your beautiful wife needs to know that they are not feminine, they are Godly.

Let your gentleness be evident to all. Philippians 4:5 (NIV)

Your queen needs to see that her king is a Godly man who hears God about the things the bible says are Godly.

There is nothing weak about helping out a person who is struggling...only a stronger person can do that. There is nothing wimpy about caring for others. It takes a powerful person to have the strength to care.

And by the way, Godly women think compassion is so sexy!

The more you show your Godly traits that you were created with, the more you will be respected for being strong enough to have compassion.

Be strong enough to be compassionate, loving, caring, empathetic, gentle, friendly and full of mercy. And always be strong enough to let your beautiful wife see these traits in you. She will love and respect you even more.

Day 21
Sit and Watch

You are an incredible woman of God. You are a powerhouse of wisdom and strength. You have been specifically chosen to compliment your wonderful husband. The two of you fit together like a hand and a glove...although it may not seem that way right now.

You have to learn to grow together. You have to learn to share. You have to learn to cohabitate.

Cohabitating technically means "living together," but it is more than just occupying the same living quarters. Living together is completely different from being together and living.

When you began dating and being pursued by this incredible man, I'm sure you never thought, "I hope someday we can just coexist in the same domicile as we pass by each other in life." You wanted the fairy tale. You wanted friendship. You wanted deep, passionate, long-lasting, head-over-heels, 'til death do us part kind of love. But somewhere along the way, that excitement for being together gave way to all the things that need to be done, and all the things that should be done, and all the things that can be done now that you and your husband are not that close.

So let's fix it. Let's get back that "Loving Feeling" that we have lost.

Your husband wants to be with you as well. Actually, he wants you to be with him, he just has no idea how to ask for it. He may not even know exactly what it is that he wants...but he wants it anyway.

He wants you by his side. He wants you to talk to him. He wants you to touch his arm as you walk by. He wants you to lean on him when he is watching TV. He can be hard and callous but your love can break through the toughest skin and as you break through, he will begin to pursue you the way he used to.

You don't have to get ooey-gooey or become needy. You just have to make it known that you are his...always, all the time, forever.

The more you subtly let him know that you are in love with him and want to be close to him, the more he will open up to you and let you in closer. Give him time to realize that you feel this way. It may not change in a day, a week or even a month...but it will.

Go in and sit by him while he is watching the game. Lean in, grab his arm and put it around you. He'll get the hint.

Remember...

Love never fails. 1 Corinthians 13:8 (NKJV).

Day 21

Dear Lord,

I come to You tonight and thank You for being strong enough to love me. Thank You for being willing to die on the cross in my place. With all the power of heaven at Your fingertips, You still yielded Yourself to death. You were strong and showed such great compassion on me even when I didn't deserve it.

Lord, teach me about being strong. Make me strong enough to show compassion to others. Make me strong enough to care more and show mercy often.

Lord, help me show my beautiful bride that You created me with these characteristics and that I recognize the strength You gave me to use them. Help me to encourage my wonderful wife to be even more caring than she is. Thank You Lord for giving me this wonderful queen, to help teach me about You and Your characteristics. Help me to bless her even more.

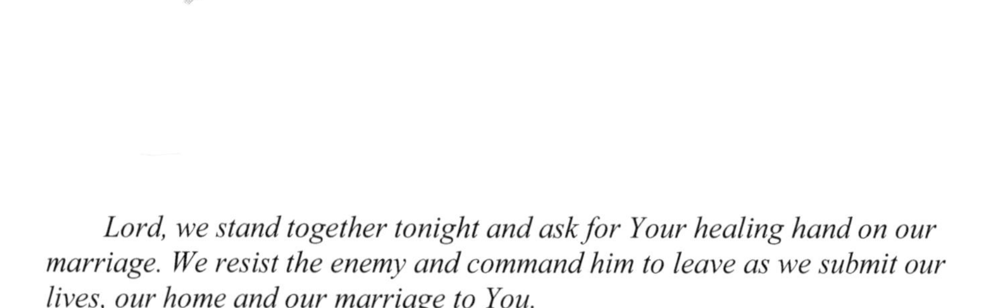

Lord, we stand together tonight and ask for Your healing hand on our marriage. We resist the enemy and command him to leave as we submit our lives, our home and our marriage to You.

We stand, praying this in the name of Your Son, Jesus Christ, our Lord; Amen.

Day 21

Dear Lord,

I come to You tonight and thank You for way You pursue me. Thank You for teaching me how to love You. Thank you for everything You gave up to come down here and sacrifice Your life so that I could live. And thank You for the time you take to be with me.

Lord, teach me about being with You. Teach me how to pursue You and how to pursue my husband. Show me how to be with him without putting pressure on him to fulfill a need in me. Teach me how to be the exact fit to what he needs in his life every day.

Lord, help me show my wonderful husband how much I love and respect him. Help me show him that I just want to be near him. Show him that his presence in my day is life-giving and enjoyable. Help me to be an encouragement to him in everything I do. Show my incredible husband how proud I am to be his queen and that I truly believe him to be my king.

Day 22
Secrets

Caution--this is where people get hurt!

We all have secrets. You want to live as an open book but you have things that you just don't want others to know about you...especially your wonderful wife. If she knew "this," she would definitely think less of me. But sometimes, it is freeing to tell her. Sometimes, it is part of your healing. You may have even received counsel to "Tell her everything."

This is dangerous ground you are on and you need to know that the enemy loves to play here. This is where people get seriously hurt. This is where you have to be very careful to know your footing but also the footing of your hurting bride, especially if what you are going to tell her is about to hurt her even more.

You are responsible for her care, not just yours. In today's society, so much is done focusing on your individual health at whatever cost. But your heavenly Father has commissioned you with a greater task. It's not about you...it's about your beautiful bride.

You do not have the right to unload all your secrets upon your wonderful wife in order to feel better about yourself. You will end up piling all your baggage upon her to try to carry and that is not the mantel that God gave her...that is actually the mantel that God gave you. This is not in any way a suggestion for you to continue to keep secrets from your precious bride. However, there is a time and way to inform her so as to cause as little pain and discomfort to her as possible. Your job is to protect her, not hurt her.

And a word spoken in due season, how good it is!
Proverbs 15:23 (NKJV)

You need to seek counsel from the One who created both you and your beautiful wife, His princess. Remember, you are ultimately responsible for how you treat this daughter of the Most High. But God gives His wisdom to those who ask and He will help you every step of the way.

Cast your burden on the Lord, and He shall sustain you; He shall never permit the righteous to be moved.
Psalm 55:22 (NKJV)

And she may have secrets too. Allow God to work in her and let her bring those to you as God leads. Don't rush her. She will be more prone to asking for forgiveness for her issues if she knows that you are ready to forgive and protect her.

Be ready...and wait on God.

Day 22
Secrets

We all have secrets and we all have things in our lives that we just don't want to share. You have things that you believe will cause your wonderful husband to think less of you. You need to know that your loving husband feels the same way. He has things in his past, in his present and yes, even in his future that already are, or will be hard to tell you.

He is most-likely going to share these things with you at a poor time. He may keep things from you until he thinks you can handle it. He may even open up and dump everything on you at once just to feel better about it himself. This can be very hurtful. You should not have to put up with him having secrets or with him revealing secrets to you that are hurtful. You should not have to put up with him doing anything wrong at all...but you do. So now what?

You have been finely crafted by your loving Father to be the perfect compliment to your husband. You can be sure that the God of all creation knew exactly what He was doing when He created you. He knew that you would be hurt. He knew that your husband would make mistakes and He created you to be able to handle this.

She is clothed with strength and dignity; she can laugh at the days to come. Proverbs 31:25(NIV)

If handled improperly, these situations can cause even more damage, to you, to your husband and to your marriage. This is where people get seriously hurt. This is dangerous ground and the enemy loves to get in here and wreak havoc. Don't let him.

First of all, believe that your loving heavenly Father knows what you are going through and is in control. He's got this. That doesn't mean that it's not going to hurt, but He's got you under His wing.

Second, believe that your loving husband wants to bless you not hurt you. He thinks he is protecting you from harm. He may be handling things wrong, but his intentions are to love you. Believe that...no matter what the enemy is trying to whisper in your ear.

Third, don't react. The enemy would love to get you and your loving husband to quickly react to every situation. If a doctor said your body was having a reaction to medication, you would worry, but if he said your body is responding to the medication, you would be comforted. Don't let the enemy make a bad situation worse by causing you to react out of fear, anger, frustration or any other emotion. Instead, take a moment and pray about how to respond. You are an incredible woman of God and secure in His love, and you know that your loving husband loves you no matter what.

Day 22

Dear Lord,

I come to You tonight and thank You for always being willing to hear me. I thank You that even when I was trying to hide things from You, You knew it all and loved me anyway.

Lord, I want to live as an open book with You, with others and especially with my beautiful wife. Help me to live my life knowing that You see everything that I do and love me anyway and help me to live in a way that my precious bride would be proud of.

Lord, You know that I do not want to share my shortcomings and my failures with my beautiful wife. I want her to think highly of me and I am concerned that she will not see me the same if she knew the real me. Help me to believe the best about her and let You be in control of her heart for me.

Lord, help me to know how and when to share all of me with her. Help me to know how to help her receive information that I have been holding back from her. Help me not hurt my beautiful wife, but only love and protect her.

Lord, we stand together tonight and ask for Your healing hand on our marriage. We resist the enemy and command him to leave as we submit our lives, our home and our marriage to You.

We stand, praying this in the name of Your Son, Jesus Christ, our Lord; Amen.

Day 22

Dear Lord,

I come to You tonight and thank You for always being willing to hear me. I thank You that even when I was trying to hide things from You, You knew it all and loved me anyway.

Lord, I want to live as an open book with You, with others and especially with my wonderful husband. Help me to live my life knowing that You see everything that I do and love me anyway and help me to live in a way that my amazing husband would be proud of.

Help me to believe the best about my wonderful husband and help me to let You be in control of his heart for me.

Lord, help me to handle any situations that come up that are hurtful for me, my marriage and my husband. Help me to respond in Your way to these situations instead of reacting. Help me to resist the enemy when he lies to me about my loving husband. Help me to always believe the best about the wonderful man of God You gave me. Let me forgive and be a help to him as he is hurting from the attacks of the enemy. Lord, I ask You to bless my loving husband and teach me to always be a blessing to him.

Day 23
...With Understanding

We have all heard this phrase. You may have even had it thrown in your face a time or two.

Husbands, likewise, dwell with them with understanding,
1 Peter 3:7 (NKJV)

But what if you don't understand what understanding means?

God has called you to be the leader of your home, the king of your castle, the ruler of your domain...but you need help. God knew this and sent you a wonderful helper. She is specifically designed to be a huge help to you.

But as you treat her like everybody else, she will feel neglected.

As you hold her to the high standard to which you hold yourself, she will feel inferior.

As you treat her like a simple helper, not as important as yourself, she will feel like a lower-class citizen.

Your commission, your directive, your mantle of leadership is not just for you to be successful individually but for you to make your beautiful bride successful. It's not just about you reaching the goal, but for you to lead your wonderful wife and family across the goal.

Your queen is to be understood as a weaker vessel but not a lesser vessel. She is a joint heir in the kingdom with you and no less important or inferior to you. The term weaker vessel may imply a physically weaker person, but it in no way means spiritually weaker. She may be your greatest connection to God and sometimes even your only connection to Him.

Understand how the Creator of the entire universe feels toward his most precious daughter. He designed her just the way He wants her to be. He made her beautiful. He made her soft and gentle. He made her intelligent and loving and then He chose a great man to love and protect her...you.

As you continually remember that she is God's beautiful princess, and you realize the way He looks at her, you can begin to see her in the same way. Tell yourself every morning that you have been specifically chosen by the King of kings and the Lord of lords to watch over His favorite daughter. Then go and tell her how honored you are to be her husband. The more you understand about her beauty, her identity, and her heart; the more she will begin to understand who she is in Christ. The more she understands her identity in Christ, the more she can understand you and your love for her.

Understand the way God created you and the way He created your beautiful bride. Hold her up in prayer and love. Love your beautiful, amazing, wonderful woman of God and treat her with understanding.

Day 23
Bad Decisions

It's no secret. We all know it's true. Everybody is talking about it. Your husband makes mistakes and bad decisions. Its official...he is not perfect.

God has called you, commissioned you and empowered you to support your wonderful husband in all areas of his life. This does not mean that you don't have a say in what happens, when it happens and even how it happens. You absolutely do. You are a very important part of this union and God planned for you to be blessed in your wonderful marriage.

However, your incredible husband has been given the mantle of leadership and he wants, expects and needs your support...even when he makes mistakes. He needs you to believe the best about him. He needs you to think that he is smart, capable and a fantastic leader.

You may disagree with decisions he makes, but how you handle the disagreement can set your marriage on a course of repairing the failure or a course of strife between you.

Your loving husband should never uncover you in public. You should be protected and secure that you can trust him as your leader, your lover, your best friend. Because you are one, he should stand by you.

In the same way, you cannot uncover your wonderful husband. You have to stand by him through thick and thin. You have to support him no matter what. Your incredible husband has to know that he will be completely protected by your love and that no danger is coming at him from you.

Your beauty... should be that of your inner self, the unfading beauty of a gentle and quiet spirit, which is of great worth in God's sight. ...the holy women of the past who put their hope in God ...submitted themselves to their own husbands.
Peter 3:3-5 (NIV)

Just because you shouldn't uncover him in public doesn't mean that you have to bite your tongue and never say anything. You are his chief counsel and best friend. He needs you to help him lead you and your family.

This is when you get to show your disagreement through your love and support...by doing it safely and properly. After the situation has occurred, you can get alone with him and let him know that he was wrong. You can tell him what you think and you can tell him what you expect.

He may not ever appreciate that you disagree with him, but he will come to understand that you disagree with him without ever uncovering him in public and he will love that. He will know that you have his back in any situation and that he can trust you to protect him but that you are still going to be honest with him about his mistakes. He will see your love, even in his bad decisions.

Day 23

Dear Lord,

I come to You tonight and thank You for always treating me with understanding. Thank You for always overlooking my shortcomings and forgiving my failures. I thank You Lord for gently holding me up as I am weak.

Lord, help me to stand strong in Your strength and to act as You would. Help me to understand what it means to treat my wonderful wife with understanding. Help me to treat her the way You treat me; always forgiving, always loving, always pursuing and always understanding.

Lord, help me to see her as my greatest gift and understand that You gave her to me, not as my possession but as my queen. Help me to understand her and her feelings. Help me to understand how to help her, how to lead her and how to bless her.

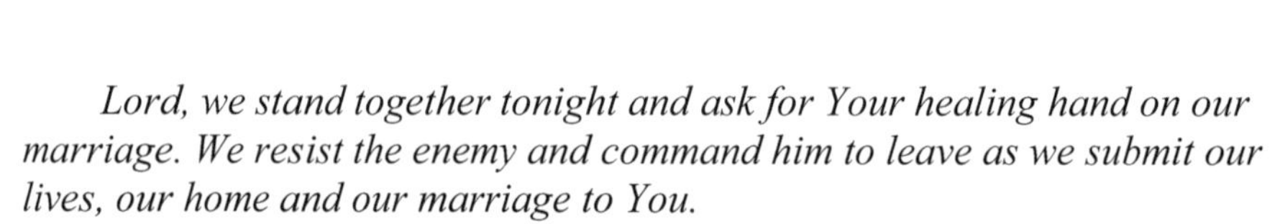

Lord, we stand together tonight and ask for Your healing hand on our marriage. We resist the enemy and command him to leave as we submit our lives, our home and our marriage to You.

We stand, praying this in the name of Your Son, Jesus Christ, our Lord; Amen

Day 23

Dear Lord,

I come to You tonight and thank You for always loving me and forgiving my failures. Thank You for always overlooking my shortcomings and gently holding me up as I am weak.

Lord, help me to stand strong in Your strength and to act as You would when I have a disagreement with my wonderful husband. Help me to treat him the way You treat me when I make bad decisions.

Lord, help me to see him as my greatest gift and understand that You gave him to me as my king. Help me to support him as I would support You in everything. Help me to always remember that You are in control and that You love me and my incredible husband. Help me to understand how to help him, how to follow him and how to bless him.

Day 24
Submission

You had to know this was coming. You can't have a Christian marriage book without covering the topic of submission; but don't assume this chapter is all about her...it's not.

But I want you to know that the head of every man is Christ, the head of woman is man, and the head of Christ is God. I Corinthians 11:3 (NKJV)

You are called to be under authority, the authority of Christ. This authority doesn't hinder you and what you want to do, have or become. This authority is actually liberating; setting you free to grow, reach, love, express and live life more abundantly.

Submission is not giving up everything that makes you uniquely you. You are not being asked by God to be some kind of puppet. He created you just the way He wants you and when He looks at you, He smiles. He loves your creativity. He loves your passion. He loves your thoughts and ideas and how you experiment and implement those ideas. He loves to let you learn and grow without micro-managing you. He loves you.

Submission is realizing that the best place for you in life is right where He wants you to be. He has your best in mind and if you can "submit" to His leading, He will lead you into success. He created you to succeed.

The better you become at submitting your life to Christ, the easier it will be for your wonderful wife to understand submission to you. She will see how you submit your life to God and she will be able to see a real world example of proper submission...and you can't really expect your beautiful wife to begin to understand submission to your leadership until you learn to submit to God's.

But another amazing blessing comes from you submitting your heart and life to Christ's authority...it teaches you how to act, how to live, how to love when someone submits to your authority. You now have an example in Christ of the proper way to be in authority. It is no accident! God designed it this way. Your marriage is a picture of your relationship to Christ. As Christ submitted to God's authority, it allowed you to have a perfect picture of how to submit to His authority; which in turn allows you to understand how to relate to your beautiful bride as she submits to you.

Don't focus your life on how to get your wife to submit to your authority...just submit yourself to Christ's authority and let God show your wife what she needs to see through you. The more you are submitted to Christ's leadership, the more successful you will become and the easier it will be for your gorgeous wife to follow you in submission.

Day 24
Submission

Well you had to know we were going to cover this topic. You can't really have a marriage book without discussing submission. But before you roll your eyes and assume you already know what we are going to say...let's look at this a little different.

You already know that your husband is your leader. You have heard about how he is in charge and the authority and responsibility for where this family goes is all on him. Yes, you are told to submit to him and yes, God expects you to do just that...but what does God say to your loving husband?

God actually tells him a lot. He tells him that he has to love you the way Christ loves His bride. He tells him how to lead, how to love and how to bless you. God tells your wonderful husband so much about how to have an abundant life, for himself and for you. It is kind of like God's never-ending training course. Your incredible husband will never stop learning as God teaches him to "submit" to His leading.

But submission for you and for your husband is not a negative thing. God is not asking you to give up everything that is special about you. God created you just the way He wants you...intelligent, unique and beautiful. He looks at you and He smiles. He loves your creativity. He loves your passion. He loves to let you learn without micro-managing you. He loves you.

Submission is realizing that the best place for you in life is right where God wants you to be. He has your best in mind and if you can "submit" to His leading through your wonderful husband, He will lead you into success. He created you to succeed.

Just like you have to learn how to submit, your loving husband has to learn as well. He is learning, sometimes the hard way, that God wants what is best for him and for you. God has a plan for your wonderful husband, for you and for your marriage. It is a plan for blessing and success.

For I know the plans I have for you, declares the Lord, plans to prosper you and not to harm you, plans to give you hope and a future. Jeremiah 29:11 (NIV)

But just as it is difficult for you to always submit to your husband, it is difficult for your husband to submit to Christ. Sure, there is the argument that it is easy for him to follow God because God is always right, but it may be difficult for him to be sure that he is actually hearing God.

You incredible husband needs your help, your support and your submission. He needs to see your example of submission so that he can learn to hear God's voice more and more. As you submit to your loving husband, he will be able to see your example and learn how to lead you as he learns how to submit and follow Christ.

Day 24

Dear Lord,

I come to You tonight and thank You for Your leadership and guidance in my life. I thank You for being my authority and being patient as I learn to submit to Your will.

Lord I ask You to help me learn to wait for my beautiful bride as You give her wisdom and guidance in submitting to me. Help me to love her unconditionally as You teach her how to be a great woman of God.

Lord, teach me what true submission is and help me to become a better man of God as I learn to submit to You. Help me to hear from You and learn from Your life about what true submission really is.

Bless my wonderful wife with Your presence as You teach her about submission and as You teach me how to lead her the way You lead me. Help me love her and be patient with her as she learns more about submission. Lord, teach me how to lead her without micro managing her. Teach me how to truly love her.

Lord, we stand together tonight and ask for Your healing hand on our marriage. We resist the enemy and command him to leave as we submit our lives, our home and our marriage to You.

We stand, praying this in the name of Your Son, Jesus Christ, our Lord; Amen.

Day 24

Dear Lord,

I come to You tonight and thank You for your leadership and guidance in life, in love and in learning how to submit to You and to my wonderful husband. Thank You for allowing me to learn how to submit to him as I learn how to submit to You.

Lord, help me to allow my wonderful husband to learn how to submit to You. Teach me how to help him and how to example submission for him.

Lord, show him that I truly love him and that I am submitted to his leadership. Thank You that I can have confidence in You as I submit to my loving husband.

Lord, I ask You to bless him as he leads me.

Day 25
Power of the Tongue

There are ways that you have hurt your beautiful wife and may not even realize it. God created her to get her highest affirmations from you and when you withhold compliments and words of affection, it can cut deep. Couple this lack with even a "soft" hurtful word from you and serious damage can occur.

Your tongue has the power of life and death within it. The words you say to your lovely wife, about your lovely wife or even about other women in front of your lovely wife can be a huge factor in the health of your marriage. But even more importantly than that, they can truly hurt your beautiful bride.

Words kill, words give life; they're either poison or fruit —you choose. Proverbs 18:21 (MSG)

So many times, we try to make ourselves look better by degrading others. This is especially hurtful when it is your beautiful bride, whom you vowed to love. It's not just the words that are hurtful but the fact that those words came from you. Your beautiful bride is there for you to protect and bless. She is designed to receive from you. You have the opportunity to give life, love and blessing, but when negative things come from you towards her, she accepts them to a much higher degree than she would from anybody else. This can cause deep wounds that can take a long time to heal.

Just as you have the power in your speech to hurt your beautiful bride, you also have the power to soothe, comfort and heal her. You have the power of life and death in your tongue...so choose life. As you speak out the words of encouragement, words of life and words of blessing over your wife, all the hurtful things you have spoken over her can be reversed. The more you speak life over your beautiful bride, the more you hear those words out loud and the more you begin to see her through those positive words of love.

The same is true of your gorgeous bride. The more she hears them, the more she will believe them and begin to step into her identity as a beautiful woman of God.

You may have noticed that we have used as many positive, loving adjectives about your beautiful wife as we could fit into this book. It was a very strategic attempt on our part to get your mind thinking in that direction about your amazing wife. We want to create situations in which you speak life over your wife as often as possible.

Protect your wonderful wife from any offenses, including the ones from your own mouth. Be very careful not to let any unwholesome talk come out of your mouth...especially about and directed toward your gorgeous wife.

Day 25
Power of the Tongue

You are so strong and powerful. You may not know it. You may not feel it, but you are. You have the power of life and death in your words.

Your wonderful husband is uniquely designed to be affected by your words in a greater capacity than anybody else. God created him to get his highest affirmations from you. When you speak blessings over him, it actually empowers him to become the man of God that he was created to be. He needs to hear those words. The more he hears them, the more he will begin to believe them. God gave you that super-power over your husband.

But you also have the power of death in your words. As you speak hurtful words to your husband, over your husband and about your husband, those words cut deep. Because your loving husband is designed by God to get his greatest counsel from you, your words carry much more weight than those of any other person on earth.

Words kill, words give life; they're either poison or fruit —you choose. Proverbs 18:21 (MSG)

Your wonderful husband cares so much more about the way you see him, feel about him and think of him than he does anybody else, or even everybody else. Even if it appears that he doesn't care what you say; even if it appears that he is not listening to you; he is taking it all in; and he is probably allowing the harsh words you have said to weigh more than the loving words...its a normal occurrence. He wants you to be impressed, but it is always easier for him to believe that you are disappointed. So your words of life have to be greater, stronger and more plentiful.

The more you speak words of encouragement and life about your husband, the more you hear them too. As you hear these things about him, the positive affirmations will begin to drown out the voice of the enemy, and the more you hear them, the more you will begin to believe them. The more you believe them yourself, the more power they carry as you speak them out to your wonderful husband. Then he will begin to weigh your affirmations with greater weight than the hurtful words you used to speak.

You may have noticed that we have used as many positive, loving adjectives about your amazing husband as we could fit into this book. It was a very strategic attempt on our part to get your mind thinking positively about your incredible husband. You are already speaking life over your incredibly amazing husband.

Protect your amazing husband from any offenses, including the ones from your own mouth. Be very careful not to let any unwholesome talk come out of your mouth...especially about and directed toward your wonderful husband.

Day 25

Dear Lord,

I come to You tonight and thank You for the way You always speak life over me. I thank You for the loving words that You say and the way You always encourage me.

I ask You to forgive me for the words that I have spoken over my beautiful wife. I ask You to heal her from the wounds that my words have caused.

Lord, help me be careful with my words and always speak life over my wonderful wife. Help me be careful to not hurt her with the things that I say. Help me to always remember that she is standing with me and not against me. Lord, help me protect her, even from my own hurtful words.

Lord, help me to encourage her with the things I say about her and about others. Help me control my tongue about anything that might cause her pain. Help me be a great protector of my beautiful bride in everything that I do and say.

Lord, we stand together tonight and ask for Your healing hand on our marriage. We resist the enemy and command him to leave as we submit our lives, our home and our marriage to You.

We stand, praying this in the name of Your Son, Jesus Christ, our Lord; Amen.

Day 25

Dear Lord,

I come to You tonight and thank You for the way You always speak life over me. I thank You for the loving words that You say and the way You always encourage me.

I ask You to forgive me for the words that I have spoken over my wonderful husband. I ask You to heal him from the wounds that my words have caused.

Lord, help me be careful with my words and always speak life over my incredible husband. Help me be careful to not hurt him with the things that I say. Help me to always remember that he is standing with me and not against me. Lord, help me protect him, even from my own hurtful words.

Lord, help me to encourage him with the things I say about him and about others. Help me control my tongue about anything that might cause him pain. Help me be a great protector of my amazing husband in everything that I do and say.

Day 26
Prophetically Speaking

Your amazing bride is an incredible helper, counselor, encourager, lover and friend. She was specifically designed to be just that amazing. So many factors in life have drained her of her ability to step into her true destiny. We have already discussed how your words have had influence in this area as well. Now let's realize that you have the power to change your beautiful wife. You have the power to help her step into her calling.

Your beautiful bride is always ready to accept words of affirmation from you...it is how she was designed by her loving Father. She wants to hear your words of love, your statements of appreciation and your prophetic blessings over her.

But so many times, your wonderful wife is not acting so wonderful. She may not be the most helpful and she may not be the most encouraging. She may not even be a good friend. So are you lying when you say she is a wonderful wife if she really isn't?

Absolutely not!

God... calls those things which do not exist as though they did;
Romans 4:17 (NKJV)

We are to do the same. This is a direct calling for all husbands to empower their amazing wives. This is your chance to cause your wonderful bride to step into the destiny that God has called her to.

As the authority over her, you are designed to speak life into her. You have the right and the authority to prophetically speak blessings that will come to pass. God made you the king of your kingdom and under His authority; you get to declare what is and what is not in your kingdom. Your queen lives under your authority and will flourish under your prophetic words about her.

As you speak the truth over your beautiful wife, all of heaven agrees with you. Actually, you are agreeing with heaven. You have been given the authority and power to speak over your incredible wife the life-giving words that God already says are true about her.

Speak out how beautiful she is and she will become more beautiful.

Speak out how loving she is and she will become even more loving.

Speak out how blessed she is and she will become even more blessed.

Your wonderful bride is a gift from God to you. She has been given to you to love, cherish and bless with all that is in you, including your words.

Speak wonderful prophetic words over your wonderful wife every day and enjoy helping her become the wonderful woman of God that she was created to be for you.

Day 26
Prophetically Speaking

Your wonderful husband is an incredible leader, provider, facilitator, lover and friend. He was specifically designed to be just that wonderful. But this world that we live in seems to wear us down in so many ways and your wonderful husband is no exception. He was created to live above the fray and yet you see him struggling to survive in so many ways.

This is your opportunity to step into your role as his helper, counselor and love of his life. As we have discussed, you have the power of life and death in your words. Your harsh words can cut deep. Your encouraging words can really lift him up. But what do you do when your husband is not acting like a good leader. Maybe he is not stepping into his role as a wonderful lover. Maybe he is even a bad friend. Are you lying when you say he is a wonderful husband if he really isn't?

Absolutely not!

God... calls those things which do not exist as though they did;
Romans 4:17 (NKJV)

We are to do the same. This is a direct calling for all wives to empower their husbands. This is your chance to cause your wonderful husband to step into the destiny that God has called him to. As you speak the truth over your incredible husband, all of heaven agrees with you. Actually, you are agreeing with heaven. You have the power to speak into your amazing husband the life-giving words that God says are already true about him.

Speak out how wonderful he is and he will become wonderful.

Speak out how blessed he is and he will become blessed.

Speak out how sexy he is and he will become sexy.

Your loving husband needs to hear these prophetic words of blessing spoken over him. The more he hears these things, the more he will begin to believe them and then he will begin to step into the destiny that God has called him to...a destiny to become a wonderful father; a loving husband; a great leader; a man of integrity; a thoughtful, caring person.

God has placed you into this relationship with all the authority to command these things into existence. You and only you have been designed to speak deeply into the heart of your incredible husband. He has been specially crafted to hear you in a deeper way than anybody else on earth.

Your wonderful husband is a gift from God to you. He has been given to you to love, encourage and bless with all that is in you, including your words.

Speak wonderful prophetic words of life over your wonderful husband every day and enjoy helping him become the wonderful man of God he was created to be for you.

Day 26

Dear Lord,

I come to You tonight and thank You for the prophetic words You have spoken over me. Thank You for raising me up with Your words of life and speaking the truth about me even before I could see it about myself.

Lord, I ask You to teach me how to speak prophetically about my wonderful wife. Teach me how to speak the truth about her and raise her up to be the woman of God that You designed her to be.

Lord, help me know the words to say about her that You say are true. Help me to always be an encourager and always speak life over my beautiful bride.

Lord give her grace to believe the blessings that I speak over her and help her to see You in the prophetic words I say.

Lord, we stand together tonight and ask for Your healing hand on our marriage. We resist the enemy and command him to leave as we submit our lives, our home and our marriage to You.

We stand, praying this in the name of Your Son, Jesus Christ, our Lord; Amen.

Day 26

Dear Lord,

I come to You tonight and thank You for the prophetic words You have spoken over me. Thank You for raising me up with Your words of life and speaking the truth about me even before I could see it about myself.

Lord, I ask You to teach me how to speak prophetically about my amazing husband. Teach me how to speak the truth about him and raise him up to be the man of God that You designed him to be.

Lord, help me know the words to say about him that You say are true. Help me to always be an encourager and always speak life over him

Lord give my amazing husband grace to believe the blessings that I speak over him and help him to see You in the prophetic words I say.

Day 27
Honoring Her Parents

There is a subtle, yet extremely important principle that God implemented for our good. Actually, it is not that subtle, we just don't pay attention to it. It is one of the 10 commandments and it comes with a promise.

Honor your father and mother...so that it may go well with you and that you may enjoy long life on the earth. Ephesians 6:2,3

When you were married and vowed to love, honor and cherish your beautiful bride, that vow included doing everything it takes to make her the best child of God that she can be. The two of you became one and her parents became your parents as well, and so you need to honor her parents even if she is not. You need to lead in this in order for you to be blessed, for your marriage to be blessed and for your wonderful wife to be blessed.

We all have a past and many of us feel as though our parents may have failed us in some way. Whether your lovely wife feels this way or not is actually irrelevant. It is now your job to lead her into living a long, blessed life. It may take time to overcome the damage she feels that she received from her parents. Take this opportunity to bless your beautiful bride by honoring her parents. As you lead in this, she will be able to walk in the blessing under you and she will begin to be healed of all the issues that are still causing her pain. You need to be the one to lead her into healing with her parents by always honoring them.

You don't need to try to get her to honor them. You don't need to argue with her about whether they are good or bad parents. Let God do His job as you do yours in honoring the parents of the beautiful woman of God that has been given to you.

This does not mean that everything that they say is correct, or that they should have a say in how you run your family. It does not even give them the right to disrespect you. It simply means that in spite of anything they may say or do, you will respect and honor them with the things that you do and the things that you say about them, whether in public or in private and especially in front their daughter, your beautiful bride.

You need to honor the fact that they have given their daughter to you to take care of and the best way you can show them that you are up to the task is to show them respect and show them that you are submitted to God in honoring them as your parents.

Show your amazing bride that you truly love her by honoring her parents...not because they deserve it, but because it is what is best for your incredible wife. The blessings on her will be immense as she lives a long blessed life with her protector, provider friend and lover...you!

Day 27
Honoring His Parents

One of the most important principles that God set out is unfortunately one of the principles that we take for granted the most. It is one of the 10 commandments and it comes with a promise.

Honor your father and mother...so that it may go well with you and that you may enjoy long life on the earth. Ephesians 6:2,3

When you agreed to marry that incredible man who had your heart, you actually were saying to God that you would do whatever it takes to make him into the best son of God that he could be. One of the best ways you can minister to your wonderful husband is to honor his parents.

He may have a wonderful relationship with his mom and dad. He may not like them at all. And whether or not you like them is not the issue here. God commands us to honor our parents and now that you two are one, his parents are now yours as well. This is not a negative thing at all. It is an incredible opportunity for you to bless your amazing husband by showing him, and his parents that you truly honor and respect them.

You do not need to try to make your incredible husband honor his parents. You don't need to argue with him about whether they are good or bad parents. God will be reaching into your loving husband's heart and showing him how to treat his parents. You just need to continue to honor and respect the parents of the amazing man of God that has been given to you as a gift.

This does not mean that everything that your new parents say is always going to be correct, or that they should have a say in how your family is operating. It does not even give them the right to disrespect you. It simply means that in spite of anything they may say or do, you will respect and honor them in the things you do and the things that you say about them, whether it is in public or in private and especially in front of of their son, your wonderful husband.

Honor the fact that they have given their son to you in marriage and the fact that God has chosen you to be a part of their family. As you honor and respect his parents, your quiet, gentle submission to God will have an enormous effect on your incredible husband. Not only will he see your attitude and actions, but he will also begin to see his parents differently, as they begin feeling and responding to the respect they are being given.

Show your amazing husband that you truly love him by honoring his parents...not because they deserve it but because it is what is best for your incredible husband. The blessings on him will be immense as he lives a long blessed life with his helper, encourager, friend and lover...you!

Day 27

Dear Lord,

I come to You tonight and thank You for teaching me to honor my parents. Thank You for the example that You have put before me in so many others. Lord, teach me how to honor my parents and how to honor my wonderful wife's parents.

Lord, help me to lead my beautiful bride in honoring our parents. Help me to honor her parents no matter how I feel or what I may think about them. Help me to honor her parents and always treat them with respect whether they deserve it or not. Help me to recognize that by honoring them, I am honoring my beautiful bride and staying true to the calling You put on my life..

Lord, help me to lead my wife into healing from her past by helping her honor her parents. Help me to know exactly what to do and what to say at each moment that would show honor to her parents.

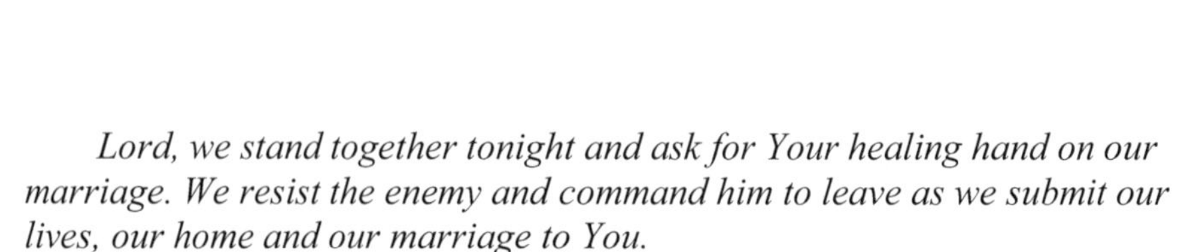

Lord, we stand together tonight and ask for Your healing hand on our marriage. We resist the enemy and command him to leave as we submit our lives, our home and our marriage to You.

We stand, praying this in the name of Your Son, Jesus Christ, our Lord; Amen.

Day 27

Dear Lord,

I come to You tonight and thank You for leading me into honoring my parents. Thank You for the example You set for me to follow.

Lord, help me to always remember that my loving husband and I are one and that his parents are now my parents.

Lord, teach me how to honor my parents and how to honor my wonderful husband's parents. Help me show them love and respect as I would my own parents, no matter how I may feel or think of them. Allow me to not take up any offense against them, but to see them through Your eyes.

Lord, help me to always remember that I do not honor them because they deserve it, but because I honor my incredible husband by honoring his parents.

Lord, help me know the depth of the relationship that my husband has with his parents and teach me how to truly help him love and respect them even more. Help me to see any hurt that there may be and be able to lift him up to You for true healing.

Lord, let my honor and respect for my parents and for my wonderful husband's parents be a sign that points to You and Your love. Help me to live in the calling that You have placed upon my life by honoring my parents.

Day 28
Praying in a Mother in the Faith

You get most of your high counsel from your beautiful bride. She gets most of her high counsel from you. Perfect...right?

Well...almost. You probably do not have a wealth of counsel about how to be a good wife to you. And on many subjects, your counsel is probably biased. This is where you can really bless your wife by praying for her to have a great Mother-in-the-Faith.

Your wife needs to learn the wisdom that God has sent to so many other women who have walked this road before her. There are so many wise, Godly women that have made mistakes and avoided issues in life that would love to be a voice to your wife. You need to begin to pray for God to send the right woman to mentor your wife, in love, in marriage and in so many other ways...it's called discipleship and we all need it.

By looking at them (older women), the younger women will know how to love their husbands and children, be virtuous and pure, keep a good house, be good wives. Titus 2:4-5 (MSG)

Don't get offended when your wife hears good counsel from somebody else instead of you. Don't allow the enemy to cause an issue here. This is a great place for you to be in charge of your marriage and commission good, Godly women to help your beautiful bride. You don't need to try to control it, just turn it over to God, who has your precious wife's best interest at heart. He will bring the right counselor and friend for her at just the right time.

Trust God to place your wife in the hands of the right woman that will bless her. Don't worry about her getting bad counsel; just keep praying for this woman of God, He will handle the rest. He will teach your beautiful bride how to hear, how to learn and how to distinguish good counsel and bad counsel.

God will protect your wonderful wife and your marriage by speaking directly to her during this time. She will begin to grow and experience God in new ways that He wants her to have. She will be learning how to follow you better, how to support you more and how to love you deeper. She can learn things from a godly woman that you cannot teach her, and she needs these things.

One day, she will have her own group of women that are looking to her because they want the kind of marriage and the kind of loving, praying husband that she has; and it will be because you were a great leader and yielded to God to find the right women to help your beautiful bride.

Trust God and begin asking Him to provide your lovely wife with a great mentor, a good friend, a Mother in the Faith.

Day 28
Praying in a Father in the Faith

You are an amazing source of wisdom for your incredible husband. God has designed you in just that way. You see things from another angle and you hear things from your heavenly Father, that are to bless your loving husband. You are his most important counsel.

Although you have a wealth of counsel to give, you may not be the best source of information on things he still needs to know. And simply because your incredible husband wants you to think he is incredible, he may have difficulty accepting counsel from you. He is trying hard to impress you. This is a fantastic opportunity to expand the breadth of your counsel. You need to allow, and even call in men of wisdom for your husband.

There are so many men that have come before your incredible husband that would love to help him be a better leader, protector, lover and friend to you. Your husband may never ask and he may not even realize the importance of having great fatherly counsel from a Godly man, but he needs this...it's called discipleship.

For by wise counsel you will wage your own war, and in a multitude of counselors there is safety. Proverbs 24:6 (NKJV)

As his chief counselor, you are commissioned with the privilege of recruiting more help for your wonderful husband. But you don't actually have to do any interviews. You just need to pray. God already knows who would be the best advice for your husband in every situation. As you pray for good leaders to come into your amazing husband's life, God moves on your behalf to bless him with good counsel.

The more you hold your incredible husband up to God to bring great counselors into his life, the more you husband will glean from these men and learn to treat you well, learn to love you more, and learn to lead through this tough life of uncharted terrain. He needs to hear from those Fathers in the Faith that have already traveled this road and can help him avoid the pitfalls that they know exist.

You do not need to make your wonderful husband to meet with these men or call anybody and tell them that your he needs help. All you need to do is pray. Pray for your husband, pray for these men, and pray that God would bring the right men into your wonderful husband's life.

As your husband learns to lead, love and live a blessed life with you, he will at some point have the wisdom and experience to pass on to other young men who need a father in the faith; young men who want a blessed life like his; young men who want a blessed marriage like his; young men who want a closer relationship with their own beautiful bride; and it will be because you prayed this into existence.

Day 28

Dear Lord,

I come to You tonight and thank You for leading and guiding me. I thank You for the counsel that I receive from my wonderful wife and thank You that she is so open to receiving from me.

Lord I ask You to send a great mentor for my wonderful wife. Send someone that she can relate to and open up to. Send someone that can be straight forward and honest with my precious bride and would be able to hear her heart and understand the difficulties that she has in being married to me.

Bless her with the right person to connect with so that she can grow even stronger in her faith, in her hope and in her love.

Give my beautiful wife discernment to know what counsel to take and what counsel does not line up with Your word. Bless my amazing wife with a great woman to be a mother in the faith to her.

Lord, we stand together tonight and ask for Your healing hand on our marriage. We resist the enemy and command him to leave as we submit our lives, our home and our marriage to You.

We stand, praying this in the name of Your Son, Jesus Christ, our Lord; Amen.

Day 28

Dear Lord,

I come to You tonight and thank You for always leading and guiding me. Thank You for the wonderful man that You have given me to follow and support.

Lord, I ask You to send great fathers in the faith to bless my husband with leading and counsel. I ask You to bless my incredible husband with wisdom from men that have learned to walk with You and are perfectly suited to help him be successful in everything that he does.

Lord, help me to always be an encouragement to my wonderful husband and to continue to remember that he needs mentors to help him on this journey of learning how to lead me. Help me to not take up an offense when he needs to get counsel from others and can't hear it from me.

Lord, help my amazing husband hear and understand the counsel that You are sending him. Help me to continually pray for him to have good fathers in the faith to teach him how to lead me closer to You.

Day 29
Praying For Her Friends

You are a great friend.

Even though you are a great friend, your precious wife needs women that she can relate to...and you may not like all the friends that she comes up with, in fact, there will almost definitely be friends that you do not like. But telling her that you do not like her friends might create tension between you and make your relationship more difficult.

This is your opportunity to pray in good friends for your wonderful wife. Your prayers will be heard because you have a mantle of authority over your marriage. It is your calling to watch over, protect and lead your beautiful bride. This authority that you have been given allows you to pray with authority over your amazing wife and the friend's that she has in her life. You can simply petition God and all of heaven goes to work to protect and bless your beautiful bride.

The effective, fervent prayer of a righteous man avails much.
James 5:16 (NKJV)

Pray for God to bring good friends into her life and for Him to remove any negative influence from your precious bride. Praying in good friends for your beautiful bride is a fantastic way to bless her. It will surround her with like-minded, Godly women who love their husbands and will encourage her to love you more.

You do not need to focus too much on her friends that you do not like. You don't need to make a huge issue with her about her friends. Just pray for good friends from God for her and God will take care of it. He may choose to remove people from her life or He may cause them to become a blessing for her. Either way, God wants what is best for her. He wants to bless her and He wants your relationship with her to be all that it can be.

God wants to give us good gifts and friends are good gifts.

As your beautiful bride grows in life with good friends, she will have opportunities to bless others with her friendship. She is a wealth of wisdom and love because God created her to be. She needs to have friends and to be a friend. She becomes more loving and wise as she is able to use the gifts that God has blessed her with to help others. She is designed to be your friend and as she learns to be a better friend to others, she will become an even better friend to you.

Bless your wife with the gift of friendship by praying in good friends for her.

Day 29
Praying For His Friends

You are a great friend. You are perfectly designed and created to be a great friend to your wonderful husband. God planned for the two of you to be friends for the rest of your life.

So why does your husband need other friends?

He may have friends that you do not like. He may have friends that distract your wonderful husband from you. Or he may have really great friends that just don't allow him to put your marriage first.

This is a fantastic opportunity for you to bless your wonderful husband by praying for his friends. He may not ever know that you are doing it, but it can have enormous effects on your husband, on your marriage and even more importantly, on your relationship.

As you begin to pray for those people in your wonderful husband's life, all of heaven begins to move to protect and bless him with good friends. God has given you this authority as your loving husband's chief counselor, supporter and encourager...as his wife.

You have position of authority over your marriage and you can call upon God to bless your incredible husband with Godly friends and to remove any negative influences in his life. God may choose to take these people out of your incredible husband's life or He may decide to change them and make them into the kind of friend's that will bless your husband and empower his relationship with you.

Be anxious for nothing, but in everything by prayer and supplication, with thanksgiving, let your requests be made known to God. Philippians 4:6 (NKJV)

You don't have to confront them yourself. You don't necessarily have to tell your loving husband how much you disapprove of his friends. You can simply pray. Allow God to work in your husband and it may show him what is best for him, what is best for your relationship and especially what is best for you, his beautiful bride.

God wants to give you and your wonderful husband good gifts, and friends are good gifts.

As your amazing husband experiences good friendships, he will learn to be a good friend. He is designed to be your best friend for the rest of your life and learning how to be a good friend is very good for your relationship.

Bless your wonderful husband with the gift of friendship by praying in good friends to build him up and encourage him.

Day 29

Dear Lord,

I come to You tonight and thank You for the gift of friendship. I thank You that You call me friend and that You teach me how to be a good friend. I thank You that my wonderful wife is my best friend and that she counts me as her best friend.

Lord I ask You to send more friends to my wonderful wife and provide her with good, deep relationships with Godly women. I pray right now for the friends that she will be getting in the near future and ask that You bless them. May they be blessed and be a blessing to my precious wife. I ask that they get blessed by the relationship with my wonderful wife.

Lord, I pray that You would draw those friends away that mean to harm or distract my beautiful bride from You or her relationship with me. I pray that You would replace them with great friends that will sharpen her and push her closer to You and to me.

Lord, we stand together tonight and ask for your healing hand on our marriage. We resist the enemy and command him to leave as we submit our lives, our home and our marriage to You.

We stand, praying this in the name of Your Son, Jesus Christ, our Lord; Amen.

Day 29

Dear Lord,

I come to You tonight and thank You for the gift of friendship. I thank You that You call me friend and that You teach me how to be a good friend. I thank You that my amazing husband is my best friend and that he counts me as his best friend.

Lord I ask You to send more friends to my incredible husband and provide him with good, deep relationships with Godly men. I pray right now for the friends that he will be getting in the near future and ask that You bless them. May they be blessed and be a blessing to my wonderful husband. I ask that they get blessed by the relationship with my incredible man.

Lord, I pray that You would draw those friends away that mean to harm or distract my fantastic leader from You or his relationship with me. I pray that You would replace them with great friends that will sharpen him and push him closer to You and to me.

Day 30
Praying for Her

You need to pray for your beautiful wife.

This book is just a starter. It is designed to get you going in the right direction and create momentum so that you can continue loving, praying and battling for your beautiful bride's heart.

Your marriage is not over and your mantle of leadership is not either. You have to keep fighting. Keep your shield up and your sword drawn, ready for any attack from the enemy against you, your marriage and especially your lovely wife. You cannot lay down your sword and rest until the enemy is defeated. You need to pray for your wife all the time, not just at night before bed.

The good news is that the battle becomes easier. The more you resist the enemy, the easier it becomes to resist him the next time he attacks. And you are building trust, so you now have another warrior, a woman of God standing next to you, fighting at your side.

How could one man chase a thousand,
or two put ten thousand to flight, Deuteronomy 32:30 (NIV)

You have broken the ice with this book and it is no longer weird to pray for your wonderful wife, alone or in front of her. So keep it up. She needs you to cover her, to protect her, to encourage her and to love her. She needs you to pray for her.

When she is sick, let your prayers be the first line of defense. Let her have confidence that God is aware of her condition because you have the authority in your family to cover her and rebuke sickness.

When she is stressed about work, life or anything else, pray for her. She will know that you care enough to take her issues to God with her.

Pray for her while you are not together as well. You have the authority to cover and protect your wife while you are apart. Keep her strong and safe by faithfully placing your loving wife in God's capable hands. He will answer your prayers and bless her while you are away.

The effective, fervent prayer of a righteous man avails much.
James 5:16 (NKJV)

There is no better way to connect your heart with your beautiful bride, than to pray for her.

Day 30
Praying for Him

You need to pray for your incredible husband.

This book is just a starter. It is designed to get you going in the right direction and create momentum so that you can continue loving, praying and battling for your wonderful husband. You have to keep fighting. Keep your shield up and your sword drawn, ready for any attack from the enemy against you, your marriage and especially your incredible husband. You cannot lay down your sword and rest until the enemy is defeated. You need to pray for your husband all the time, not just at night before bed.

The good news is that the battle becomes easier. The more you resist the enemy, the easier it becomes to resist him the next time he attacks. And you are building an amazing, trusting relationship, so you now have another warrior, a man of God standing next to you, fighting at your side.

How could one man chase a thousand,
or two put ten thousand to flight, Deuteronomy 32:30 (NIV)

You have broken the ice with this book and it no longer feels weird to pray for your wonderful husband, alone or in front of him. So keep it up. He needs you to stand by him, to support him, to encourage him and to love and respect him. He needs you to pray for him.

When he is sick or stressed, let your prayers be the first line of defense. Let him have confidence that God is aware of his condition because you have taken your request to God for his healing. You operate under the authority given to you by Christ and your loving husband, and therefore have the power to rebuke sickness from your family.

Pray for him while you are not together as well. That ring on our finger gives you the power to act with authority over your entire family, including your husband. The enemy has to acknowledge your rightful position. You have the authority to cover and protect your incredible husband even while you are apart. Keep him strong and safe by faithfully placing your loving husband in God's capable hands.

The prayer of a righteous person is powerful and effective.
James 5:16 (NIV)

There is no better way to connect your heart with your wonderful husband, than to pray for him.

Day 30

Dear Lord,

I come to You tonight and thank You that I am always on Your mind. I ask You to keep my wife always on my mind in the same way.

Help me to think about her while we are apart and help me to pray for her. Bless her with Your presence and keep her safe and strong.

Help me to continue to be the man of prayer that You designed me to be. Help me be a great leader and prayer warrior for my beautiful bride and bless her even when I get distracted with work or life.

Lord, keep me focused on being my wife's leader, lover and king. Help me lead her the way You lead me. Help me love her the way You love me and help me to be her godly king as she is my beautiful queen.

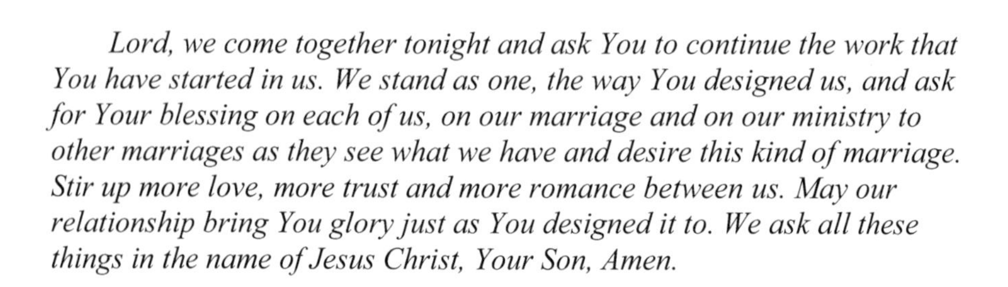

Lord, we come together tonight and ask You to continue the work that You have started in us. We stand as one, the way You designed us, and ask for Your blessing on each of us, on our marriage and on our ministry to other marriages as they see what we have and desire this kind of marriage. Stir up more love, more trust and more romance between us. May our relationship bring You glory just as You designed it to. We ask all these things in the name of Jesus Christ, Your Son, Amen.

Day 30

Dear Lord,

I come to You tonight and thank You that I am always on your mind. I ask You to keep my husband on my mind in the same way.

Help me to think about him while we are apart and help me to pray for him. Bless him with Your presence and keep him safe and strong.

Help me to continue to be the woman of prayer that You designed me to be. Help me be a great helper and prayer warrior for my incredible husband and bless him even when I get distracted with work or life.

Lord, keep me focused on being my husband's helper, lover and queen. Teach me to be the kind of helper that You designed me to be for my wonderful husband. Help me love him the way You love me and help me to be his Godly queen as he is my incredible king.

You did it!

You just completed *The 30 Day Marriage Challenge!*

Some interesting things happened to you, to your incredible spouse, and to your marriage.

First: You have been blessed. You may not even feel it but God is faithful and...

...he rewards those who earnestly seek him. Hebrews 11:6 (NIV)

Second: Your spouse has been blessed. You have been praying for them. God is moved by your faith and has poured out blessing on them because of your prayers.

The effective, fervent prayer of a righteous man avails much.
James 5:16 (NKJV)

Third: Your marriage has been blessed. You have been praying every night for your marriage and your prayers change things. But you have also been taking some other powerful steps:

--Holding hands with your spouse every night.
--Dedicating time every night just for them.
--Looking them in the eyes every night and saying, "I love you."
and...
--Creating a habit of all of these things.

You can now continue to pray for and in front of your spouse and it no longer feels weird. You can say, "I love you" and it doesn't sound awkward.

You can speak prophetically over them all the time, not just at night and watch them become the amazing child of God that He intended.

If you are still uncomfortable in any way, just repeat The 30 Day Marriage Challenge again. This time, expand your prayers to what God is putting in your heart every night for your spouse.

Shout Your Love to the World...

or at least tell us.

Now that you have completed *The 30 Day Marriage Challenge*, we would love to hear about your experience. We have been praying for you and your marriage and the feedback we get really is a blessing. We love hearing about the things God is doing and how we can continue to be a part of it.

Please email us and let us know about you and your relationship and what has changed. Be as general or specific as you would like and you don't even have to put your name. We never sell, rent or even distribute the information; we simply like to know that we have been a part of what God is doing.

Be sure to tell us all the important details such as how long you have been married, how you met and how much you love each other.

Contact us at:

BradandLaura@Bethel1808.com

Do you need to talk?

Maybe you just need somebody to listen to you and your spouse.

Maybe it's not too serious.

Or maybe you are at the end of your marital rope.

There is a wonderful ministry for your marriage, it is completely free and you do not need to be a member of a church to be blessed by this ministry.

You will not be asked to join any church and your session is confidential.

It's called Marriage Challenge and it is a ministry of Gateway Church in Southlake, Texas.

You can set up an appointment to meet with another couple, who has been where you are. You are not the first couple to have problems and Marriage Challenge is set up to pair you with those that have already traveled this road.

There is hope.

There is victory.

There is a great marriage in your future.

Contact Gateway Church, Southlake Texas.

GatewayPeople.com

Do you need some more encouragement?

Would you like to hear our story?

Do you like watermelon?

If you answered yes or no to any of these questions, check out our first book...

Goodnight Gorgeous, by Brad C. Engel

It is an incredible story of how God can take any marriage and turn it into an incredible blessing.

From a bad situation to a great marriage...Goodnight Gorgeous is a heartfelt, true story that is filled with practical advice and lots of humor.

Available at Bethel1808.com

Also available in print and digital versions at Amazon, Barnes and Noble and everywhere great Christian books are sold.

About the Authors

Brad and Laura Engel were high school sweethearts. An accidental overdose of passion created a very bad situation which neither of them were prepared to handle.

Entering into marriage with tons of baggage and an idea that they could conquer the world and live on love; created a path that kept them together while breaking their hearts. Scratches and cuts would tear at the love that they thought they had and years went by with the idea that it would somehow get better. It got worse.

But God is good!

Brad and Laura are honeymooning in their 31st year of marriage, 17 of which have been "Happily Married."

Brad is an author and public speaker working with companies across the nation and Laura is a Biology and Anatomy & Physiology teacher in high school.

Their entire story can be found in:
Goodnight Gorgeous, by Brad C. Engel

Contact Brad and Laura and let them know your story after you have completed the challenge. Reach out to Blessed@Bethel1808.com.

Made in the USA
Columbia, SC
20 April 2019